THE DA OF ˉ MISSISSIPPI RIVER

The story of the dalesmen and their families who went from the Swaledale area of England's North Yorkshire in the early part of the 19th century to seek a new life in the country of the Upper Mississippi River

THE DALESMEN

OF THE

MISSISSIPPI RIVER

by

David Morris

William Sessions Limited
York, England

ISBN 1 85072 062 2

Printed in 11/14 Times Typeface
By William Sessions Limited
The Ebor Press
York, England

Acknowledgements

IN THE PREPARATION OF THIS BOOK I have received invaluable assistance from many sources and my thanks are due to all those who have helped with information and advice. Some must be given particular mention.

Dr John Thornton Dixon now of Newcastle College for his earlier extensive work in the field of emigration from the dales and for his important thesis 'Aspects of Yorkshire Emigration to North America'.
Michael D. Gibson, Archivist of the Center of Dubuque History, Loras College, Dubuque.
Loren N. Horton of the State Historical Society of Iowa.
The Galena/Jo Davies County Historical Society.
Dr Stafford M. Linsley of the University of Newcastle Upon Tyne.
The Maritime Records Centre, Merseyside Maritime Museum, Liverpool.
The State Historical Society of Wisconsin.

Louie Allan of Ripon for Harker family records.
Harold Beadle of Richmond for advice in mining matters.
George Buxton of Ashford, Middlesex for access to family letters and photographs.
Stephen Calvert of Benton for much information and proof reading.
Donna M. Caygill of 527 Franklin Street, Box 261, Linden, Wisconsin, 53553.

Joseph C. Harker of California.
Alfred Mueller of Galena, Iowa.
Geoffrey Pratt and other members of the Pratt family.
Margery Raisbeck of Harrogate, Yorkshire.
Richard J. Vincent of Galena, Iowa, for his knowledge of the early lead mines and providing many mining photographs.
The many people in the dales who have provided information and encouragement.

Julie Dodd of Richmond, North Yorkshire for map drawings.

D. M.

Prologue

IT WAS OCTOBER WHEN I travelled through Wisconsin and reached the great Mississippi River. I was bound for the old city of Dubuque, a name conjuring up stories of America's Mid-Western history, the Sauk and Mesquakie Indians, the Winnebagos and the astute French traders, particularly Julien Dubuque, who gave his name to this settlement of earlier times.

I had come from Yorkshire in England following the trail of others who had gone long before. They were the many lead mining and farming families who had journeyed some 150 years ago from their tiny villages in the Yorkshire Dales seeking a new life in the developing limestone area of the Upper Mississippi valley. Some I knew had reached Dubuque in 1834, if not before, and as I looked across the city, the October sun lit up the brick buildings, the busy riverboats and particularly the spires and buildings of the churches. If I was to follow a trail of history, it was surely to the churches I must go.

Visiting a church graveyard is hardly a cheerful way of spending your day. But during my stay in Dubuque and in my subsequent travels in Iowa, Grant, Lafayette and Jo Davies counties, the gravestones seemed all to have their own story to tell. They gave me the names of many original immigrants to this area, the English, Welsh, Irish and a few Scots, together with some from other parts of mainland Europe. But in the centres of the early lead mining, there were many, many families and individuals who had come to America from one particular part of England's Yorkshire Dales, and that was the Swaledale area. In visiting Dubuque, I was perhaps following in the footsteps of a respected Yorkshireman, James Lonsdale Broderick, the son of a Swaledale family. He visited the city in 1876 and wrote in his diary of meeting many immigrant families from the dales who were well settled in the area.

Dubuque today had still much history to tell me. But the time came to leave, and after I had crossed the Mississippi into Wisconsin, I was much rewarded by an invitation to stay in the home of a Swaledale descendant, Stephen Calvert, in the village of Benton, known at one time as Cottonwood Hill. There I was able to talk to many good people whose forebears had come from the Yorkshire Dales as immigrants. From Benton I was taken to visit the sites of a number of early lead mines like the highly productive Champion Mine, which Swaledale men did much to develop, and others which carried the name of individual Swaledale families. Then to places like New Diggings, Mineral Point, Leadmine and Platteville, which were so much a part of mining in the last century. At Galena on the old Fever River to the south, there was more history to be related, for this was the base from which much of the mining industry east of the Mississippi was developed.

There could only be one sequel to my visit. Here was a story which needed to be told; a story closely linked with events in English history and with the development of America as a nation. To tell the story is to endeavour to place on record the experiences of many humble Yorkshire emigrant families who began leaving their villages in the 1820s to make new homes in America. They were mainly mining folk, hardworking and thrifty people who came to play no small part in developing and continuing the mines of the Upper Mississippi limestone area. The majority settled, they mined and they smelted ore, and in time they became established farmers. Many had large families, and they continued to play a purposeful role in the life of a unique part of the Middle West. They have many descendants in the America of today.

D. M.

Contents

Illustrations

CHAPTER I

An Introduction to Swaledale and its People

THE ENGLISH WRITER ELLA PONTEFRACT, who well knew the Yorkshire Dales of her time, described Swaledale as 'a little country in itself'. Few who have been there would disagree. Shut in by a barrier of the Pennine Hills in North Yorkshire and remote in its setting, it is a beautiful valley which follows the course of the River Swale downwards from the high hills, past villages like Muker and Gunnerside, which were Norsemen settlements, to the township of Reeth, of Anglo-Saxon origin. Here it is joined by Arkengarthdale, and with its new tributary the Arkle, the Swale flows down to the old market town of Richmond with its Norman castle standing guard over the entrance to the dale.

The people of Swaledale have for long been a closely knit community, strong in character and resilient in their way of life. Their neighbours in Arkengarthdale, though smaller in number but independent in their outlook, developed a mutual interest with Swaledale in mining the local deposits of lead and, for this reason alone, we may be allowed to treat the two peoples as one. Farming has always been important in Swaledale and more so to the people of the neighbouring Wensleydale. There, some important lead mines were developed, but in this wider valley of the River Ure, agriculture was generally of prime importance. Lead is said to have been mined in lower Swaledale in Roman times and perhaps even earlier in history, and though farming was for many centuries the main occupation, mining was to become more and more important. Indeed, by the middle of the 17th century, a considerable local industry began to develop which was to provide lead mining work for an increasing population for over 200 years. The rise and ultimate fall of the lead mining industry during this important period of Swaledale history is recounted in a later chapter; suffice to say that, when recession came in the late 1820s, an increasing number of families were living in a state of poverty and it was all too clear that the worsening economy just could not provide a living for the number of people who had made their homes in the area.

As the impact of real poverty began to take its toll, a gradual exodus of people, particularly from Upper Swaledale, became inevitable. The first phase of migration had begun by 1830, and of those first to leave seeking a new livelihood elsewhere were many of the more recent incomers to the dale. Those without mining or farming work and with no other means of subsistence left to look for work in the mills of Lancashire, South Yorkshire or in the coalfields. But amongst many of the younger members of the more established dales familes, there was much talk of emigration to America. There, it was said, lead mines were being developed and there was good farming land available for settlers. Moreover, working people enjoyed a political equality which gave them an opportunity to lead a much better life than in Britain.

It was of course easy enough to deliberate and talk about ways of getting to the New World. But to make the decision to break away from their roots and leave their families and friends, probably forever, was much more difficult. And yet gradually a few came to accept that there was no real alternative and, whatever the risks involved, they must go and seek a new life across the Atlantic. They were to become the dales pioneers, men and some women who began leaving the area in the 1830s or earlier and made their way to Liverpool, hoping to find a boat destined for America. By 1852 a considerable number of people had gone from Swaledale and Arkengarthdale and some from Wensleydale. Then, for some 20 years, because mining conditions in the dales improved and the Crimean war began, there was a general lull in emigration. In the early 1870s, however, there was a further downturn in lead mining and a new exodus of emigrants, which was to last until the end of the century and beyond. They went not only from the Yorkshire Dales but also from the lead mining areas of Durham and Northumberland.

But this is the story of those who left in the earlier days. The prospects they had to face were certainly daunting, to say the least but they were men and women of considerable courage. Few if any of them would have had much experience of life outside their village areas, and it is unlikely that any had ever even seen the sea. Certainly, crossing the Atlantic in the steerage of a sailing ship was no journey for the faint hearted. The story of these strong willed and determined dales characters is based on letters written at the time and on records, published books and other information kindly made available by museums and private sources on both sides of the Atlantic.

It is a story which has its roots not only in the demise of the lead mines in Yorkshire, and the Swaledale area in particular, but also in the experiences and hardships of centuries of dales life which shaped the character of those who sought to find work and new homes in America. To know something of the early experiences of these peoples and perhaps to understand how their resilience and strength of character must have developed, let us take a brief look at a few centuries of their earlier history.

CHAPTER II

Some Swaledale History

ROBERT PEACOCK MUST HAVE HAD an eye for business. Described in the records of his time[ø] as a lead merchant, he lived in Arkengarthdale around the year 1300. Like his fellow lead merchant, Alan Gill, he probably had a farming background, but with access to lead supplies, he must have found it worthwhile to take packhorse loads down to Richmond, where there would be buyers for lead in the market.

Richmond at that time was a busy market town. Following dreadful devastation at the time of the Norman Conquest, the 12th and 13th centuries had seen a new era of building and commercial trading. Lead was much in demand for roofing and other building work, and it was being exported through the Port of Yarm on the River Tees and by way of Boroughbridge to York and the Humber. Indeed, the worth of the lead deposits in the dales had been known long before Robert Peacock and Alan Gill began trading in the Richmond market.

For some time, the monastic presence in Yorkshire had been considerable, and, in particular, the monks of the Cistercian Order, who had come from the pastoral country of the Cote d'Or in France, were practised farmers and good administrators. They

---

[ø] VCH YKS (2), Assize Roll 1060 m31d.

1 *An early photograph of Richmond Market with the Keep
of the Norman Castle in the background.*

built great monasteries like Rievaulx and Fountains, and they developed a most extensive sheep farming organisation which influenced the whole area, including Richmond and the dales. However, the monastic influence was beginning to wane even in the time of Robert Peacock and Alan Gill. Changes were soon to come, and a series of events in the 14th century and beyond brought recession and hardship to the whole dales community.

Firstly, there came a succession of bad farming years, mainly because of some of the worst weather local people had ever experienced, and this created a shortage of food. Then there were repeated raids by the invading Scots who robbed and pillaged the whole area, only Richmond itself being able to buy itself out of trouble. To make matters worse, there came the Black Death and several plague epidemics. Between the years 1349 and 1374, the town of Richmond lost a considerable proportion of its population, and the villages of nearby dales did not remain immune from these and later epidemics which developed in the area. It was certainly a difficult period in Yorkshire history.

Agriculture in the dales had been at a low ebb for many years, but by the middle of the 16th century there were some signs of improvement, and small groups of men continued to mine lead in parts of Swaledale and Arkengarthdale; yet with the poor standard of living, poverty and disease being ever present, times were still extraordinarily hard for the dalesfolk. Moreover, the early part of the 16th century was to bring yet new problems. In 1509, the Tudor King Henry the Eighth came to the throne. He was soon to start putting the English Church under government control and to begin the first stage of its establishment as a national church. But the Dissolution of the monastic system and the reforms that went with it were by no means universally accepted. In Swaledale, as elsewhere, there was fear that the transfer of monastic lands to the Crown would result in increased rents and depress the already low standard of living. Resentment came not only from the local tenants but also from the big landowners who felt that their powers were being undermined by the government.

The unrest which followed led ultimately to a rebellion in 1536 which became known as the Pilgrimage of Grace. As far as the local people were concerned, it was a rebellion just as much against poverty and social conditions as for any religious reasons. In an effort to bring peace, the King offered a pardon to the leaders of the rebellion, and many of the gentry accepted. But there were those in the dales like the Swaledale landowner Sir Francis Bigod of Healaugh who remained suspicious of the King's intentions and continued to rebel. Sir Francis was soon captured and, having incurred the wrath of the King, he was beheaded, as were others who had continued the rebellion. One of the leading rebels in the area of Swaledale and Arkengarthdale was another Peacock – Anthony – who, following disturbances in nearby Barnard Castle, was ordered to be hung on Richmond Moor[Ø]. He was a victim of the process of retribution demanded by Henry the King and enforced by Thomas Cromwell and the Duke of Norfolk.

In 1558, Elizabeth the First – Good Queen Bess – came to the throne, and at last a period of comparative prosperity began to develop. The Queen was a Protestant and a woman of strength and subtlety. But during her reign she had to contend with strong Catholic support in the North and certainly some continued resentment arising from the Dissolution. She is well remembered in history not only because of the many problems created for her by the Catholic Mary Queen of Scots but also the victory she was later to achieve over the Spanish Armada. But during her reign, the Queen did much to encourage and rejuvenate trade and to show concern for the welfare of her people.

In an indirect way she brought help to the people of the Swaledale area by her encouragement for the wearing of stockings rather than the hose previously favoured. From this change of fashion developed the hand knitting of stockings, and with local wool available, nearly every dales family became involved in some way with the business of knitting. There were middlemen, known as hosiers, like Henry Atkinson, Thomas Gill, John Peacock, Anthony Pratt and John Spensley, names which were later to become known in the American Middle West. These hosiers procured the local wool, farmed it out to the knitters and collected the finished knitting for subsequent sale. It was said that miners used to knit on their way to work; certainly knitting was regarded as being part of the daily routine by many wives and even by their children. Though payments for this work were small, a great many dales families regarded knitting as a means of earning useful and often essential additional income. The stockings and hats produced found a ready market not only in Britain but also in

[Ø] Letters and Papers of Henry *VIII*. 1537-416.

2   *Martha Dinsdale of Appersett knitting with four curved
needles and using a knitting stick.*

countries like Holland. It was a trade which was to continue for over two centuries and has been revived in recent times.

Following the Dissolution, monastic land in the Swaledale area was leased out to tenants, and a system of open-field farming encouraged crop growing. This was gradually replaced by enclosures and a change to pastoral farming. Farms tended to be larger in the lower parts of Swaledale, but in the higher areas there were established yeoman farmers like the Brodericks and the Garths, and in Arkengarthdale the Peacocks had a considerable presence. Though the size of farms was enhanced by access to moorland grazing, a system of divisible inheritance meant that few holdings passed through many generations without being divided. In consequence, a number of smallholdings were created which, over the years, enabled many dales families to keep above the poverty level.

CHAPTER III

The Rise and Fall of an Industry

DURING THE REIGN OF QUEEN ELIZABETH I, demand for minerals had increased and lead mining in the dales had been given encouragement by a respected group of traders, the Merchants of York. Indeed, one of their number was another Robert Peacock, an alderman of York and for some time Lord Mayor, and he is said to have arranged for the shipment of Swaledale lead to the Baltic Port of Danzig. From the middle of the 17th century the whole lead mining operation in Swaledale, Arkengarthdale and Wensleydale began to develop into an industry requiring organisation, more modern methods and capital investment. No longer would local men think of lead mining as a sideline to farm work, as had been the case in earlier times.

The major part of the mining operations in this area was to come under the control of influential owners like Lord William Powlett, Lord Wharton, Dr John Bathurst and his son Charles, and several companies, like the London Lead Company, came to be established to finance and extend mining in the dales. There were major developments along the north side of Swaledale running through into Arkengarthdale, particularly in the general area of the Old Gang Mine, and there were other mines and smelters at Grinton and at other points on the south side of Swaledale. Though there was lead mining in Wensleydale, at Grassington, and several other places in Yorkshire, the mines of Swaledale and Arkengarthdale were said at one time to be producing about half of all the lead produced in the county and a sizeable proportion of the total mined in the whole Northern Pennines.

The mining developments in the Swaledale area could be described as an early form of industrial revolution, and as the whole business of mining lead assumed greater proportions, new workers and their families were attracted into the area. Some came from adjoining Wensleydale, Teesdale and other nearby dales, but others – like the Barkers, the Buxtons and later the Pratts – came from Derbyshire. The Raistricks came from the Isle of Man, though they were originally from Teesdale, and others came from Westmorland, and as far away as Cornwall. Many were to remain for generations and play their part in the life of the community.

Foremost in the minds of the mining community was the market price paid for the lead being produced and further developments in the mines in the 19th century were prompted very much by the need to produce lead at an economic cost. Certainly concern about lead prices proved to be well founded. During the Napoleonic War years, the prices remained fairly static, always above £20 per ton. But there was a dramatic fall at the end of the war, followed by a revival to over £27 a ton. As if to emphasise the fluctuating fortunes of the industry, there came a catastrophic fall during the period between 1826 and 1832, firstly to £19 a ton and then to a mere £12. There seems little doubt that the main cause of this major downturn was the import of considerable quantities of lead from Spain.

Much of this Spanish lead came from Adra in Granada where the lead deposits were of high quality and easily mined. Since the Spaniards were able to undersell other producers, the effect on the Swaledale mining industry, which had been operating well in the early 1820s was very considerable. Soon it became evident that the less productive mines had no future and before long would have to be abandoned. The others could only compete with the Spaniards by the best use of available machinery and economic mining methods. In any event, the ore which could be worked at a reasonable cost was approaching exhaustion in several of the smaller mines, and developments had to be concentrated in the richer areas of the Old Gang complex and Arkengarthdale. It was not a good omen for the miners of Upper Swaledale, where production was already beginning to run down and the leases of the smaller local mines were soon to be abandoned.

But lead mining in these dales had always been a precarious industry, and it would be wrong to give an impression of general prosperity even in the peak periods of the mining era. Though owners, investors and officials were in the main well rewarded by the industry, the earnings of ordinary miners were quite variable. Before 1820 it was common for wages to be paid only quarterly or even half-yearly, and families frequently lived on credit as a result. Though monthly payments became general, various forms of subsistence and parish relief were often needed. Many families came to find that they could only keep above the poverty level if they had access to a smallholding and some earnings from knitting. Conditions in the mines were often extraordinarily hard; lung diseases were all too evident, with bronchitis, consumption and other chest complaints taking their toll. The average age of death of those working underground was at times as low as 45 years. From the time of Queen Elizabeth I to the end of the 18th century the population of Swaledale had increased by some 5,000 and housing had become overcrowded and quite inadequate. A study of the parish records of those times confirms the poor living conditions and the extent of the poverty which existed, particularly in Upper Swaledale and parts of Arkengarthdale.

For the men able to continue in mining work despite the growing recession in the industry, earnings began to fall to about half the previous level. Miners had always been eternal optimists, always

3, 4 *The remains of some mining buildings, once part of a great local industry in Swaledale and Arkengarthdale.*

hoping that things would improve, but by 1830 the steady fall of lead prices had produced a period of unrelieved depression, made the worse by an onset of sheep disease and a fall in farming incomes. Men who had no mining work could see little promise in the future, though for a time they could just manage to exist if they had a smallholding. For others, only parish relief could save them from the depths of poverty. It was in this situation that there came the gradual exodus of young people. They left the dales against a background of despair and went to seek work and a possible livelihood elsewhere in England. But our concern here is for those dales people who had visions of a new life in another country where there was said to be mining work, good farming land and a future of great expectations.

CHAPTER IV

The Start of a Journey

1830 WAS CERTAINLY A BAD YEAR. By then the hand knitting trade could provide little relief to those otherwise unemployed, and pauperism was becoming commonplace amongst the ordinary people. In Muker Parish alone, the relief bill reached £1,000 in 1831, a considerable sum in those times. Edward Broderick, father of the diarist James Lonsdale Broderick, wrote at that time 'miners are forced to obtain a living in other countries which they cannot get here. The independence of spirit is gone'.

The realisation had indeed come particularly to the younger members of the older dales families that, with little future except poverty to look forward to, they must leave and seek a new livelihood elsewhere. Yet some who knew they must go could not bring themselves to break away from the life they had always known in the dale, and they delayed their decision. Others chose to stay and survive as best they could in the hope that conditions would improve. The more resolute, having decided to emigrate, had to rely on information which in those early times was sparse and sometimes misleading. It is certain that those we rightly regard as the dales pioneers were venturing into what was for them very much the unknown. In his writings of about 1830 Edward Broderick made clear the trauma and sadness in the dales villages when the emigrants made ready for departure. 'I had always thought favourably of America' he wrote, 'and believed they were acting wisely in going. Yet I confess that my spirits were much depressed at the thought of their long and dangerous journey and the difficulties they would have to encounter.'

There were many single men amongst the earliest groups to leave. A few who were married went with their wives, some with children, and others left their wives to follow them when work had been found and there was a home to go to in the new country. To raise enough money for their journey and for their upkeep until work could be found in America, many sold most if not all their possessions except for a mattress or straw bedding, a few clothes and a chest or other container to house their belongings during the journey. They knew that they must take food for they had heard that on most ships carrying emigrants only water and the most frugal of rations would be available. They took what they could, some oatbread, flour, dried meat, perhaps some cheese and tea. A cooking pot seemed essential, and items like candles could not be forgotten.

By the time Edward Broderick had started writing his 1830s diary, some of the pioneers had already left. One Muker man, John Harker, had emigrated in 1825 and other Harkers are known to have reached America in the 17th and 18th centuries. One of these was Anthony, who went to Boston, Massachusetts in 1633. Though little is known of these very early Harker emigrants, the records of John's emigration suggests that he was a man of intelligence and an individualist. He had heard that an English company, Powles Illingworth & Company, was recruiting workers for the Colombia Mining Association's gold mines in South America. It is evident that he applied and was accepted for the work. Little is known of his journey to Colombia but he reached the gold mining area of Santander (his story is told in a later chapter).

Amongst the number of men who left the Swaledale area of Yorkshire in the middle 1820s were Ambrose Hugill, Robert Waller and other members of the Harker family. During the following few years their number grew to include many names familiar to historians today. There were James Pratt and his wife, Hannah, who went from Gunnerside in 1833, Martin, Michael, Henry and Isiah Calvert, Metcalfe Bell and his friends Anthony Hunt and John Holmes and the ten Bonsons who travelled with six members of the Waller family. In 1839, William Harker Calvert left Thwaite in Swaledale at the age of 22. He went with a group known to include local men like Isaac Alcock, Edmund Alderson, William Atkinson, James Barningham, Matthew Blenkiron, another Martin Calvert, Isiah Gill, Simon Harker, Thomas Longstaff, and William Peacock. These men are known to have agreed to keep together until they reached their destination in the Middle West. They were only some of the pioneering dales people who left in the 1830s or before, each one resolved to find success in the New World.

They left, some with horses and carts, others only with hill ponies loaded as packhorses. When possible, wives and children rode on the carts and men not riding on horses set out to walk. Their destination was the great Port of Liverpool where it was said there were ships which sailed across the 'gert dub'*, the name they gave to the Atlantic Ocean. Liverpool was some 100 miles away and it was certainly several days journey. This they could accept, but the despair they felt with thoughts of those they were leaving behind was not helped by the uncertainty of the future.

The first part of the journey was to climb over into Wensleydale. From Swaledale many emigrants would have used the track over Oxnop to Askrigg, though some from Thwaite and Muker would

---

* The dales dialect word 'dub' means a deep dark pool in a river or stream and it is a word still heard in Swaledale. The 'gert dub' was a description of the Atlantic Ocean as a 'great deep pool'.

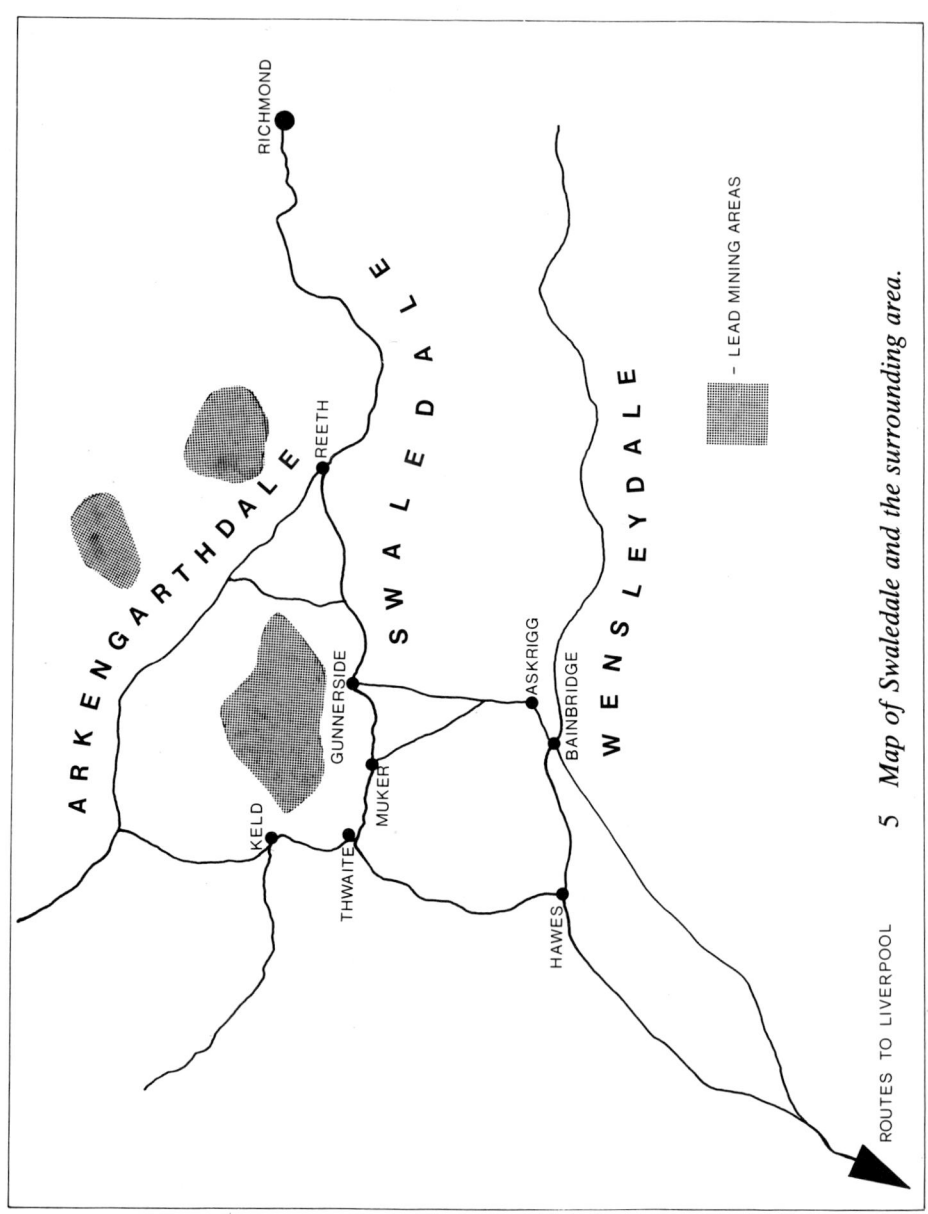

5   *Map of Swaledale and the surrounding area.*

certainly have climbed up the steep track over what was known as Stags Fell passing the Buttertubs and then down to Hawes. In Wensleydale they could join the Richmond to Lancaster turnpike. This road, built around 1751 to link the North Sea with the Irish Sea was maintained under the turnpike system by levying tolls. Though this turnpike route was really the stringing together of sections of ancient highways, it served a very useful purpose. It would have eased the travellers' journey across the Pennine Hills, and the emigrants probably were allowed to proceed without paying any tolls.

From Askrigg the road led to Bainbridge, once the site of a Roman settlement. From there a steep track made good use of the Roman route, climbing up to Wether Fell and on to Gearstone and Ingleton. But many of the travellers would have used an easier route through Hawes and on to Chapel le Dale and Ingleton. At night it was a case of seeking any available hospitality from houses on the route, sleeping in barns or under a cart, but they would have travelled as much as they could each day. After reaching Ingleton the way was clear, down the valley of the River Lune to within sight of Lancaster with its castle and church standing high above the city. 'There are trades of all sorts there' wrote Celia Fiennes over a century earlier. 'I cannot say this town seems a lazy town.'

At the time of the early dales emigrants it was indeed a busy place where over 12,000 people lived. Here was a port with ships at anchor and the emigrant travellers would have had their first sight of the sea. When John Dinsdale[ø], an emigrant from Wensleydale travelled with his family from Askrigg to Liverpool in 1849 they were able to take a sea passage from Lancaster to the Mersey and by that time there was also a railway link with Liverpool. But many other dales emigrants travelling in the late 1840s, and certainly those who went in earlier times, chose to follow the road

[ø] Diary of John Dinsdale, 1849.

6   *An impression of Lancaster in the 18th century.*

southwards to the market town of Preston. Then there were miles of Lancashire countryside to cross, until ultimately they would come within sight of the River Mersey and Warrington, an ancient town much prized by the Romans. To follow the course of the river would lead them ultimately to the Mersey Estuary with the sea beyond. Before them would be a sight they must surely have gazed at in amazement: a great forest of sailing ships. And, even from a distance, they would hear the noise and bustle of what was the famous Port of Liverpool.

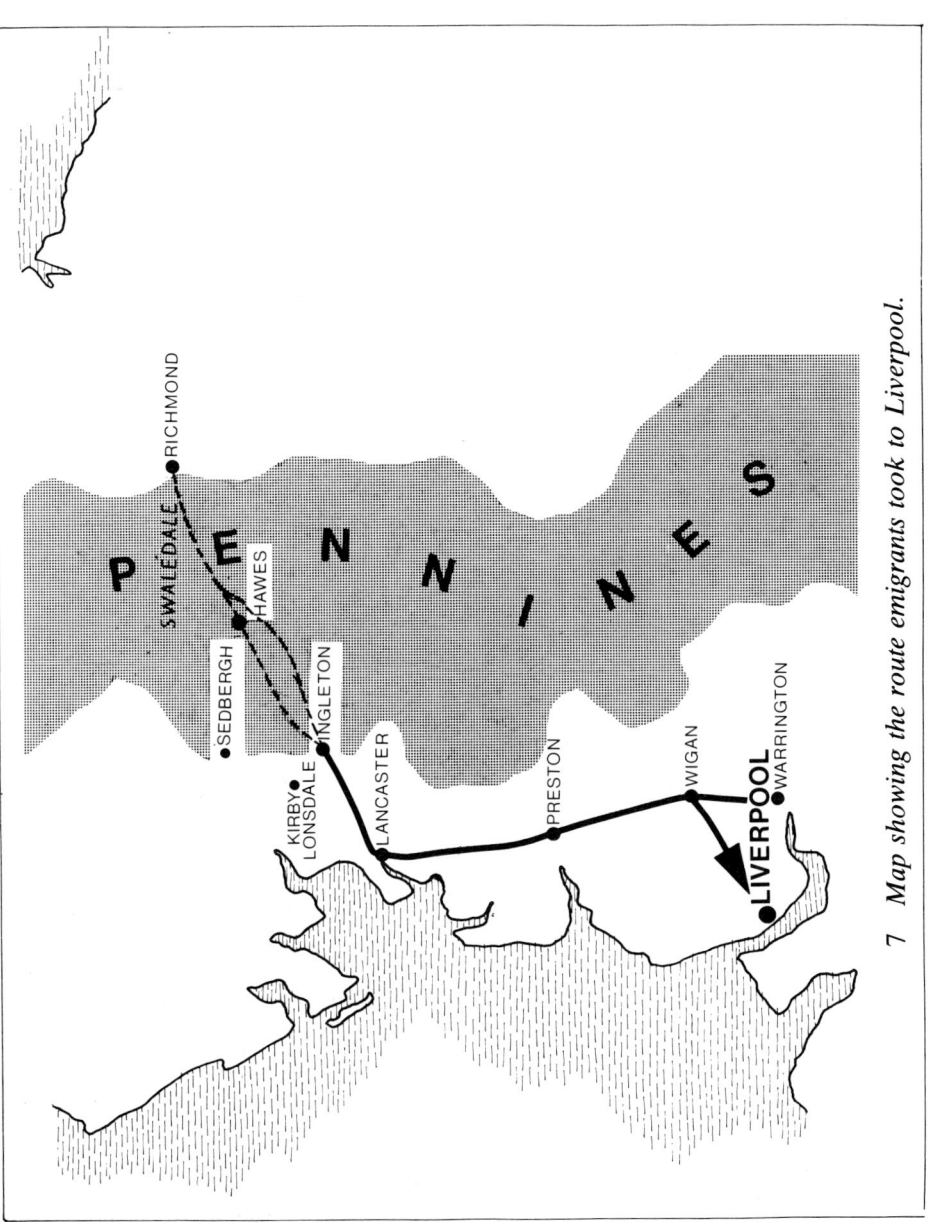

7 *Map showing the route emigrants took to Liverpool.*

CHAPTER V

A Port to Cross 'the Gert Dub'

SADLY THE FAME OF LIVERPOOL as a port now lies largely in its past. King Henry II granted the city its first charter as long ago as 1173, mainly because it gave easy access to Ireland. But it was many years later before the port began to gain any wider importance. By the 17th century the first European settlements had been made in America, and Liverpool began to play an increasing role in trade between Europe, Africa and the New World. Indeed, it

8   *The Waterloo Dock, Liverpool as it is today.*

22

came to be said that Liverpool had a larger fleet of merchant ships than any other port in the world. But disruption was to come with the conflicts of the English Civil War between the Royalists and the Parliamentarians, the troublesome days of Oliver Cromwell and the wars with Holland and France.

Liverpool soon rekindled its commercial will, and as it moved into the 18th century, the building of a customs house and new docks attracted more business, including valuable trade with India. Links with Africa, the West Indies and America involved the port in the slave trade, and this has perhaps remained as a skeleton in Liverpool's cupboard. However, it is true to say that the port's maritime prosperity had already been firmly established before any involvement in this trade, and for the most part the slaves were sent directly from West Africa to the West Indies or to the cotton and tobacco areas of the United States. Into Liverpool came cargoes of cotton and timber, and as the port continued to attract a wide range of commercial business, it became a merchanting capital, a great shipping centre and, for a time, the second largest city in England.

The great ports of the world have always been a haven for the unscrupulous, the thieves and confidence tricksters. Liverpool in the early part of the last century was no exception. Emigrants arriving at the port were met by 'runners' who would offer to carry luggage which the unsuspecting traveller might never see again. The 'runners' were aptly described by a Liverpool barrister as being 'cheats and villains like so many pirates'. Cases of bewildered emigrants being intimidated into paying excessive charges for some services were all too frequent, and there was always the traveller who passed over money in exchange for 'American dollars' which later proved to be forgeries. It was easy to become caught in a spider's web of dishonest passenger brokers and boarding-house keepers intent on extracting from emigrants as much money as possible, and travellers had always to resist paying exorbitant prices for last minute purchases made before departure. By 1850 the emigrant trade was said to have reached the peak of corruption. Even in the earlier years, the Port of Liverpool was certainly no place for the unwary, and it was into a hotbed of dockland life that the emigrants from the Yorkshire Dales had to find their way. Most got safely onboard ship, but for a few, their journey ended in Liverpool, where some are said to have settled.

Emigrants had generally to deal with a broker in order to arrange passage and steerage accommodation was always in demand as it provided the cheapest way of travelling. But there was always likely to be overcharging. Agents and passenger brokers were known to buy up the entire steerage accommodation of emigrant vessels and hold a monopoly position in the sale of passages. Fares could vary day by day, and even hour by hour, but the average steerage charge ranged from £3 to £5, male adults

9   *An impression of the dockside scene at the time of embarkation.*

having to pay the higher rate. There were always pitfalls which could make emigration difficult and sometimes impossible. There were dishonest agents who took payment for steerage passages and then absconded with the money, and it was not unknown for sailings to be indefinitely postponed because vessels were libelled* with debt.

Usually there was a waiting period of up to ten days before passage could be provided. During that time there was little alternative but to find room at one of the infamous lodging houses or to sleep rough, always guarding your belongings. Most of the lodging houses were to be found in the streets backing onto the Waterloo Dock area of Liverpool. The charges could be quite exorbitant even though the majority of these lodgings were known to be filthy, overcrowded and lacking any adequate washing or sanitary arrangements. They must have provided a foretaste of living conditions on some of the emigrant ships.

---

* The term 'libel' was in use in the last century in relation to a suit in admiralty against a vessel, its cargo or its owner.

CHAPTER VI

The Ships for the Journey

BY THE TIME THE PIONEERS FROM the dales began their travels to the New World, Liverpool was much involved in the cotton trade with the Southern States of North America, and the many ships bringing cargoes across the Atlantic were being used on the return journey for a new purpose, the carrying of an increasing number of emigrants in steerage accommodation to New York City and other American ports. There were also transatlantic packet services which began operating as long ago as 1818, and these improved considerably when steam driven vessels like the 'Great Western' came into service late in the 1830s. When Charles Dickens visited America in 1842, he made the crossing to Boston on board the 1,200-tons steam packet 'Britannia' in 18 days, despite encountering some heavy Atlantic weather. While the owners of the steam packet boats at first displayed little interest in the 'cheap-ticket' emigrant trade, with more accommodation available on their ships and the soaring demand for emigrant passages in the 1840s, they began to regard emigrants with rather more favour.

Many of the cotton ships used for the emigration trade sailed from ports like Charleston in West Virginia, Savannah on the coast of Georgia and the Mississippi port of New Orleans, returning via New York or other ports. These and other similar vessels were mostly American owned, and as they were primarily freight

10 *Emigrant families in their steerage berths.*

carriers, they had to be converted to provide for passenger carrying at the beginning of each westbound voyage. Though some were larger, many of the vessels made available for steerage passengers did not exceed 800 tons in weight and few boats were purpose built with emigrant passengers in mind. In most of these American cotton ships, the steerage passengers were 'housed' between the upper and lower decks. Often there was less than six feet between the decks, giving only a minimum of headroom. On some occasions emigrants are known to have had to exist in the dreadful atmosphere of the orlop, the space below the lower deck normally intended for heavy cargo.

To provide steerage accommodation, an area of no more than 75 by 20 feet seems to have been allocated, and on either side of a five foot aisle, double rows of rough-plank berths were built up. Each berth was ten feet long and five feet wide and was supposed to provide space for six adults, no provision being made for children. On some boats there could be four rows of berths set up to accommodate the maximum number of people. Whatever the arrangements, a steerage passage literally meant camping, usually between decks, sleeping on a wooden bunk and living for many weeks in cramped conditions. There were seldom any portholes, and hatchways, fastened down in bad weather, provided the only ventilation.

It was all too evident that the conditions on some of these emigrant ships were quite appalling and when the first Passenger Act was passed in 1803, it was intended to improve the lot of migrant travellers. In an effort to prevent overcrowding, the Act limited the number of passengers to one for every two tons of the ship's register. Later this regulation was changed in another Act to a limit of three passengers for every five tons. But these and later Acts could too easily be evaded. In the late 1840s when emigration reached a peak, dreadful experiences were still being reported by travellers arriving on American shores. Some owners were said to be sending out boats that were quite unseaworthy, and there were reports of cruelty by captains and members of the crew. It must be said, however, that many captains did the best they could to ease the overcrowding and improve the lot of their steerage passengers, but poor ventilation and quite inadequate sanitary arrangements must have made these long ocean voyages always difficult to endure.

11 *Another illustration of steerage accommodation.*

When Charles Dickens returned from America in 1842, having sailed on the packet ship Washington, he published his American Notes. In these he freely expressed his concern for steerage passengers, with particular concern shown for those unable to find a livelihood in America. 'The whole system of shipping and conveying these unfortunate persons is one that stands in need of thorough revision,' he wrote. 'The law is bound, at least upon the English side, to see that too many of them are not put on board one ship and that their accommodations are decent and not demoralizing and profligate.'

With the increase in the number of emigrants, it became the practice to appoint supervisory agents at the major ports. As early as 1832 Lieutenant Robert Law was given the important Liverpool appointment though his presence seemed to do little to improve the lot of the emigrants in those times. From America there came some recognition of the benefits it could gain by encouraging suitable emigrants to come to the New World, so early in the 1840s agents were sent to England to stimulate interest and give advice on living conditions. In the late 1840s there was a considerable escalation in emigration from European countries generally – between 1845 and 1849 well over one million Irish people are said to have emigrated. Apart from the Irish there were the English, Welsh and the Scots as well as many from Germany and Scandinavia and others from Russia. Nearly all travelled steerage.

By no means did all of these and later emigrants favour the United States. A considerable number went to Canada some of whom later travelled southwards into the U.S. Middle West. Despite the long voyage involved, other settlers began to go to Australia, taking advantage of available financial assistance; and some went to South Africa, where there was mining work. As time went on, the emigrant sailing ships were gradually replaced by steam driven vessels and an era of speedier and more comfortable travel began to develop. By the end of the last century, the Port of Liverpool had played a very major part in perhaps the greatest movement of people across the world in mercantile history.

CHAPTER VII

The Emigrants at Sea

FROM THE EARLY 1830s LIVERPOOL's Waterloo Dock became the main departure point from which emigrants like those from the Yorkshire Dales set out to board the American ships destined for New York, Boston, Baltimore, Philadelphia, New Orleans and other ports. It became the staging post, the assembly area for anxious and often bewildered emigrants wondering what the future held for them. There they had to wait with their belongings to board a sailing ship on which they would have to exist as steerage passengers for a journey of at least 3,000 miles. Many reports of the early voyages emphasise the vast concentration of shipping on the Mersey, and when the time came for them to sail out of the estuary into the channel beyond, it must have been an awe inspiring spectacle for the villagers of the dales.

Since the days of Columbus, the Atlantic passage westward was noted for rough seas and strong winds, and out in the open sea, the discomfort and the perils of ocean sailing would soon have become evident. The weather indeed held sway over the fortunes of the emigrant sailing ships, and few made the crossing to America without meeting storm force winds which were liable to prolong the voyage by 10 to 15 days. Hannah Buxton, who emigrated from Swaledale at the age of 57 years on the Saxony wrote, . . . 'We came in sight of the Welsh and Irish coasts. By this time almost all

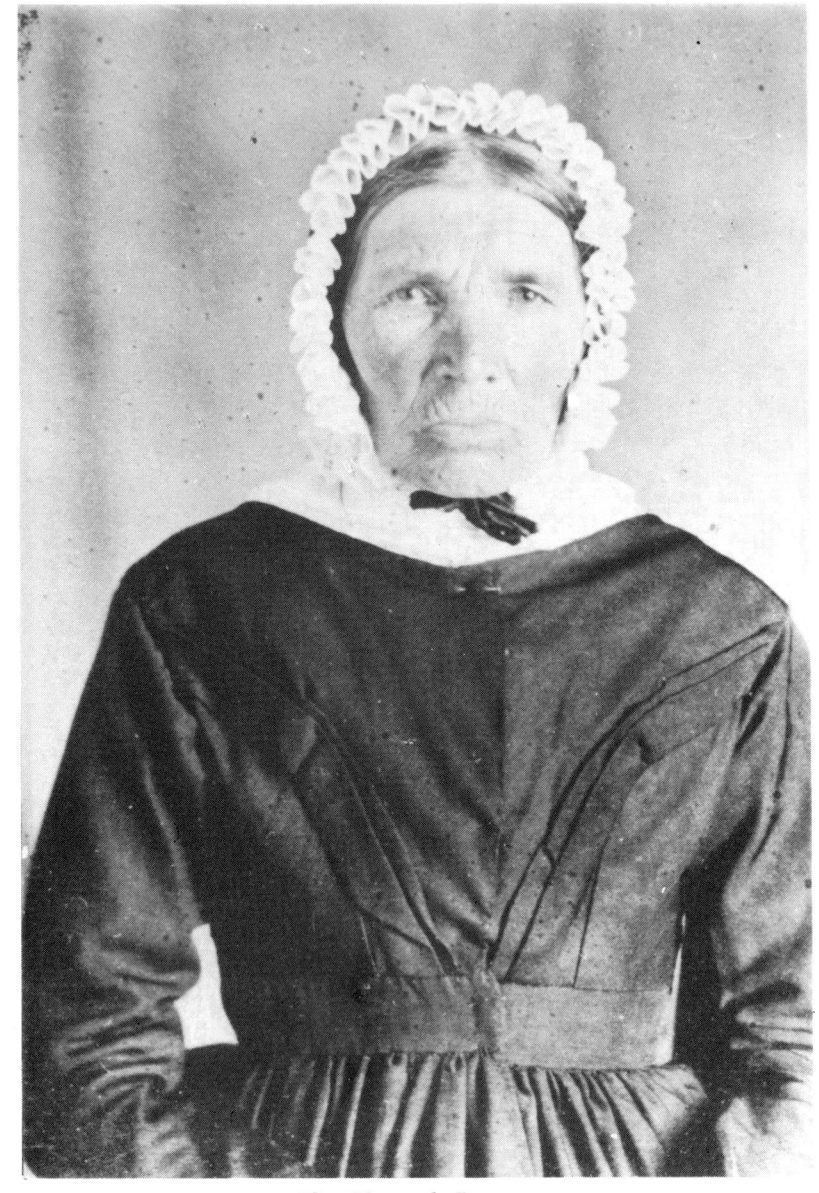

12   *Hannah Buxton.*

the passengers were sick. Two days after leaving Liverpool, the ship ran into a very severe storm and the wind continued to blow so strongly that the majority of passengers thought of no less than going to the bottom'.

The Atlantic weather could certainly be quite merciless and easily blow the early emigrant vessels off course into the Bay of Biscay. 'A storm arose', wrote an emigrant in the ill fated ship the India. 'It continued for four days and five nights. Hatches were fastened down. About midnight, a number of boxes and barrels broke loose and rolled from side to side according to the motion of the ship, breaking the water cans and destroying everything capable of being destroyed. In a few minutes, the boxes and barrels broke to atoms scattering the contents in all directions. The cries of the women and children were heart rending, some praying others weeping bitterly as they saw their provisions and clothes destroyed.'

The discomfort of steerage passengers in such storm conditions is emphasised in many reports. Children especially were very apt to suffer, as little or no provision was made for their welfare. They could only play in semi-darkness in the five-foot aisles between the rows of berths midst baggage, cooking utensils and food. Many children are known to have died on emigrant voyages, and several of the Swaledale families suffered losses in this way. During the voyage of Hannah Buxton's ship the Saxony, mentioned earlier, at least seven children are known to have died. On the other hand, the adult death rate during the early emigrant voyages was generally low, though the position deteriorated as the numbers of emigrants increased in the late 1840s.

Disease was indeed a major concern for all emigrant travellers. Dysentery was frequent, there were outbreaks of the much dreaded ship's fever, a form of typhus, and cholera was by no means unknown. The fetid atmosphere of steerage was made the worse by the oil lamps which were used for lighting and the stench of dirty bilge water. Often the defective diet of the emigrants did nothing but encourage epidemics. The emigrants themselves seemed often to have encouraged the spread of disease by their failure to observe the minimum standards of hygiene. In 1830, some passengers on the ship Jefferson bound for Baltimore from Liverpool were found to have lice which necessitated examination of all clothing and bedding. In 1831 a plague of asiatic cholera was passed on to some of the emigrant ships in Liverpool, causing considerable distress. Some emigrants were much more prone to disease than others, and those who started their journey in a poor state of health were easy targets for epidemics. This applied particularly to the Irish at the time of the potato famine when many were said to be weakened by hunger even before they began their travels.

There is little doubt that most of the pioneering emigrants of the last century were regarded by the ship owners as little more than 'return cargo'. Easy though it is to over-emphasise the problems of these men and women, it is certain that those who survived the long voyage without illness or mishap had much for which to be thankful. In many ships, medical facilities were quite inadequate to meet outbreaks of dysentery, fever or other diseases, and much depended on the ability of the captain to control infection and supply any available medicines. However, from the records available, most of the pioneering Yorkshire Dales emigrants survived the rigours of these voyages and, on reaching their American port, were able to continue their journey. But with the considerable build-up of emigration by the middle of the 1800s, demand for steerage passages intensified, standards showed little improvement, overcrowding seems to have increased, and all too often, discomfort and the danger of disease continued to bring hardship and distress. Although life for steerage passengers was always spartan to say the least, it seems likely that some of those who travelled in the peak 1840 period may have fared rather worse than did the earlier settlers.

When John Harker left Muker for the goldfields of Colombia, he was starting a journey of over 4,000 miles across the ocean. Though for those sailing to North America the distance was not as great, the problems of combating the elements were much the same. Vessels like the Hark Away of 545 tonnage which left Liverpool in 1834 carrying many members of the Swaledale Bonson and Waller families would be unlikely to have reached New York in less than 30 days, and many sailing vessels crossing the Atlantic in those times took considerably longer. A great many of these ships went into the Port of New York City; for instance, the Roscius which left Liverpool in 1839 carrying amongst its passengers some 70 dales emigrants and their children. These included William H. Calvert mentioned earlier in this book who was to return 10 years later to marry Jane Alton of Gunnerside and take her back to Wisconsin.

To avoid a long overland journey when they reached America, many emigrants came to favour the even longer ocean voyage from Liverpool to New Orleans whence they could travel up the Mississippi River to the lead mining and farming country of the Middle West. When he returned in 1849 with his new wife, William Calvert preferred this route and travelled on the Saxony together with many others from the Swaledale area. Their voyage to New Orleans took a little over two months, a long period to be confined in the prison-like steerage area common to most of the emigrant vessels. Even when they reached New Orleans, they had several weeks further travel by riverboat up the Mississippi.

CHAPTER VIII

Food for the Voyage

IT WAS GENERALLY UNDERSTOOD by early emigrants, certainly by the Swaledale folk, that very little food would be provided for most steerage passengers on board the boats leaving for America. Efforts were made by the government over the years to improve this situation, but, though some ships were much better than others, it was not until the middle of the last century that anything approaching adequate food supplies began to be available. Before then it was necessary for everyone to take sufficient food for many weeks of travelling. To help emigrants, printed guides were issued giving advice to take enough food for voyages of up to 60 days. These guides listed items of food recommended for the journey including such things as flour, rice, ginger, salt, port wine, potatoes, tea and biscuits, not to mention candles. By the time John Buxton and his 57 year old mother, Hannah, went to New Orleans in 1849, their boat provided a weekly ration of pork, oatmeal, rice, peas and biscuits, much more than is known to have been available for many earlier emigrants, who may well have received little more than water and ships biscuits to supplement their own supply of rations.

The fact that many of the early emigrants from the Swaledale area were young and well used to hardships would certainly have been in their favour, but the food they are known to have taken for their journey must generally have stood them in good stead. Perhaps the most important basic food they took was haverbread, supplies of which they packed in barrels. The name is derived from the Scandinavian 'hairi', or oats, and it provides a reminder of the Norse ancestry of a number of dales families. Haverbread, or havercake, was cooked on what was known as a 'backstone' and took the form of thick, round oatcakes[Ø]. They must have been regarded as a staple diet by many Swaledale families onboard ship.

There was always the danger of fire on the wooden vessels converted for use by emigrants, and when fire destroyed the ship Ocean Monarch shortly after leaving Liverpool, 440 people are said to have lost their lives. All cooking had to be done at a communal point on deck, but when boats were at sea in bad weather, hatches were battened down and cooking was out of the question. Passengers able to do so sometimes paid money to the ship's cook in return for help in heating food, but most emigrants had little option but to take their turn in cooking their food on deck when weather conditions allowed. There is little doubt that those passengers able to provide themselves with an adequate diet during the voyage were the most likely to keep free from illness. As has already been mentioned, there are few recorded cases of illness amongst early Swaledale emigrants other than their children.

Though the men from the dales were probably better able than many steerage passengers to survive the rigours of an Atlantic voyage, their wives not only had to undergo the traumas of the journey but, on reaching the New World, be prepared to meet all manner of hardships and uncertainty, to rear and feed large families and to labour with their husbands in creating a new livelihood. They were certainly women of great courage and stamina. Religion played a major part in the lives of these dales emigrants. They were mainly of the Methodist faith, and they are

[Ø] Ella Pontefract – Dalesman Vol. 6. September 1943.

known to have held regular services or prayer meetings during the Atlantic crossings. In America, they did much to establish new Methodist churches in the areas in which they settled, and there is no doubt that they gained much moral strength from their firm religious convictions.

CHAPTER IX

Southwards to Santander

THOUGH THEIR INROADS INTO North America were limited, the 16th century saw the Spanish and Portuguese effectively in control of the rest of the continent, the huge area of Central and South America. Not only did the Spanish empire in America have a considerable head start on the English, it is evident that by the middle of the century, the Spaniards had laid the foundations of every one of the 20 republics of Central and South America, apart from the Argentine. It was a conquest which brought a spectacular yield of treasure. As they developed control over this empire, the Spanish found an indigenous Indian population more numerous and more advanced than the English and French found in the North. Though the conquest was certainly not achieved without considerable bloodshed, the Spanish were different in that they set out to convert the Indians to the Catholic faith and then to incorporate them into their society.

In the North-West of this Spanish stronghold was an area which came to be named after Christopher Columbus; it is known to us today as the Republic of Colombia. Here, in the area of the mountains, with their considerable mineral wealth, is the area of Santander and the city of Bucaramanga. In the year 1825, a young Yorkshireman from Muker in Swaledale arrived in this Spanish speaking mining country, and his name was John Harker[Ø].

[Ø] 'The Harker Family in South America' – Charles Harker (privately printed).

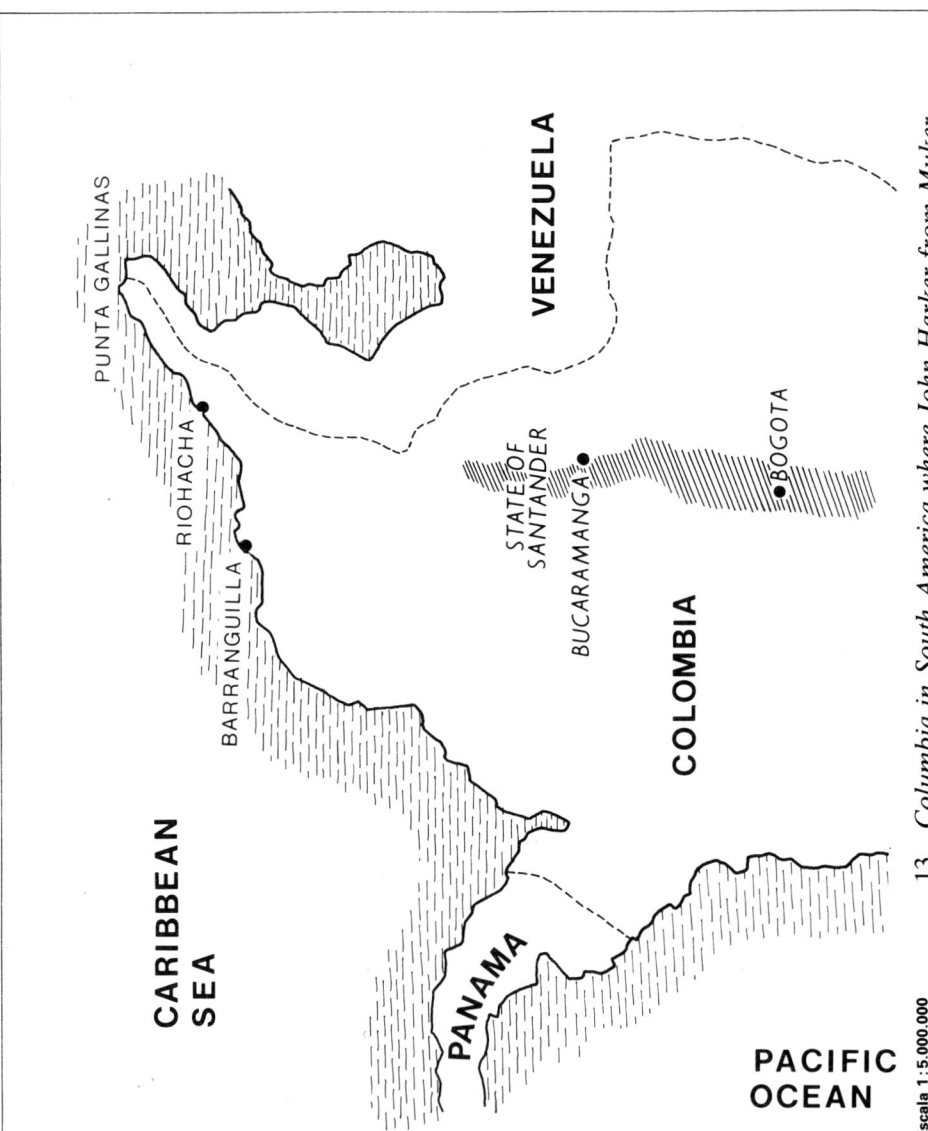

13   *Columbia in South America where John Harker from Muker*
     settled and established his family.

John came from a family established in Upper Swaledale for many generations. He was aged 21, and he had worked locally as a miner. But he must have been an intelligent young man with a desire to better himself. He was destined to seek new horizons. Correspondence of that time tells us that he visited Newcastle and probably London, perhaps to improve his education or possibly to find new work. It is known that he made contact with the English firm Powles, Illingworth and Company, who acted for the Colombia Mining Association. They were recruiting men to work in the gold mines of Colombia, and John Harker must have applied and been accepted. In the spring of 1825 he seems to have sailed from Liverpool and, though we know little about his voyage, he arrived safely in Colombia where he was soon working in the mines of Santander.

Within three years John Harker had met and married a beautiful young Colombian girl, Mercedes Mutis. She was only 15 years of age when they married and in November 1828 they had a son Don Adolf. John's employers must have thought highly of him for he was made Director of the Zipaquira mines, where he introduced great improvements in the methods of working. In September, 1829, as Superintendent of Mines, he signed a three-year agreement with the company's agents under which he was to be paid $2,500 per annum. Young Adolf went to school in Bogota and was soon shown to have above-average intelligence. But sadly, he was only 14 when his father died. Some say that, having been brought up in the Yorkshire Dales, John Harker was never able to come to terms with the Colombian climate. Whatever the cause, John was only aged 38 at the time of his death.

Adolf had been greatly influenced by his father, and in 1846 he accepted a clerkship with Powles, Illingworth, Wilson and Company. Within two years Adolf was able to converse in the English language whereupon he decided to go to England and meet his father's family. For three years, he worked with the firm

Santamaria Uribe and Company in Liverpool. In 1849 he decided to return to Colombia but, when within 200 miles of his home port of Santa Marta, he was shipwrecked on a particularly uninviting part of the northern coastline known as Punta Gallinas. In a letter written to an aunt in the Yorkshire city of Ripon he described how his vessel foundered during the night, close inshore. Both the captain and mate were drunk below decks, and the passengers and crew had to contend with aggressive Indians who swam out from the shore. They boarded and looted the shipwrecked vessel, and Adolf lost all his luggage and personal belongings. 'The Indians have taken almost everything', wrote Adolf. 'We saw thousands of them on the sea shore near the vessel, many of them drunk with the champagne sherry they had taken.'

But Adolf and his fellow passengers escaped in one of the ship's boats. 'We armed ourselves with cutlasses and muskets and coming on deck, chased the Indians from the vessel after wounding one or two. After this, we lost no time in jumping into the boat and putting the captain in by force.' Thirteen hours had passed since the ship had struck a reef. Now, having made their escape, they spent the following night and most of the next day trying to reach a friendly port. But the sea was rough and the boat was dangerously overcrowded with 16 people aboard. During the daylight hours there was little relief from exposure to the hot sun, and for food they existed on bad sea biscuits soaked in water. But fortune came their way late the following evening when they were picked up by an English tug and taken to the port of Riohacha on the Magdalena coast of Colombia. When writing to his aunt in Yorkshire, Adolf told of his return on a schooner a week later to visit the scene of the shipwrecked vessel, only to confirm that his five large cases including books and many things brought from England had been taken by the Indians and few of his belongings remained.

Adolf made his way back to his home town of Bucaramanga, where he soon began to take part in public life by being elected in

1853 to the legislature as a member for Bogota. The following year he began travelling, once more visiting England as well as France and the United States. It was on his return that he married Maria Antonia Mutis and when they had a son, he was given the Harker family name of Simon. It was in 1883 that Adolf took his son to England to visit Yorkshire, the home of his ancestors. Simon studied at Bede's College* and then spent a period with a London business house. When he returned to Colombia, it was to follow his father into government positions and to devote much of his time to youth education. He married in 1887 and fathered nine children.

When John Harker left his friends in Muker back in 1825, none could have envisaged the important role he would play in this South American country. Though he died at an early age, he had gained a responsible position in the mining industry. Moreover, he established a Colombian family of Harkers which continues to the present day. As the Historical Society of Santander has recorded, it is a family of which Santander is proud.

---

* Believed to have been St Bede's Catholic College, near Manchester.

CHAPTER X

The Arrival of the Men of the Dales

THERE WAS CERTAINLY NO GREAT welcome for the pioneering folk
from the Yorkshire Dales as they landed in New York City. It was
the main port of arrival for a high proportion of European
immigrants. Some, however, reached America by way of Quebec
and Montreal, where reception conditions in the early days were
reported as being quite appalling. There were others who travelled

14   *South Street from Maiden Lane, New York 1830.*

44

on ships destined for ports like Boston and Philadelphia and again, a growing number who took the Mississippi River route from New Orleans to St Louis and beyond.

But for a great many of the early settlers from the Yorkshire Dales, arrival in America meant setting foot in New York, a port not unlike the Liverpool they had already experienced. Here again, runners, touts and 'harpies' infested the dockland areas; robbery and fraud were commonplace, and there were the same undesirable boarding houses. It was said that corruption here was even worse than in Liverpool. After weeks at sea in steerage accommodation immigrants were checked and medically examined because there was fear that they would bring in ship's fever, smallpox or cholera. Anyone ill or needing hospital treatment received scant sympathy; and though, according to Charles Dickens, the hospitals were acceptable by the 1840s, he cannot have visited the immigrant hospital on Staten Island about which a passenger on the ill-fated ship India wrote, telling of great cruelty, meagre rations and appalling conditions. Certainly the New York hospitals in the first half of the last century did not seem able to provide proper service for immigrants needing treatment. The fact that a hospital tax came to be levied seemed to do little to improve matters.

Few agencies existed to smooth the path of the new arrivals, and it was not until 1847 that a State Board of Immigration was set up and 1855 before any proper system of immigration protection became effective. Beginning life in the New World of North America was certainly not made easy. Many immigrants had no employment arranged, and those without a trade or profession found it difficult to exist unless they had friends or relatives already established and able to give a helping hand. Some arrivals looked only for labouring work and found themselves trapped in eastern ports. Immigrants without money and unable to find work could well finish up in one of the pauper refuge centres. The Alms House

– that is to say the workhouse of New York as described by Charles Dickens – provided for some 1,000 poor people. 'It impressed me, on the whole, very uncomfortably,' he wrote. 'New York is a large town and a great emporium of commerce where good and evil are intermixed'. There were of course some immigrants who, in the end, could see no future for themselves in North America, so, if they were able, they joined the ranks of those who returned to Europe. But for the great majority, America presented a land of wonderful opportunity and hard work, and the will to create a satisfying new life eventually brought just rewards.

The established merchants of New York welcomed the immigrants as a lucrative source of employment for their shipping, although on the other hand, the authorities always feared pauperism amongst the incomers. Any immigrant who increased the drain on available relief funds was therefore far from popular. Once new immigrants arrived, it became the policy to 'keep them moving' out of the area. Nevertheless, many were to settle, the Irish in particular, and the population of New York continued to grow and became more and more cosmopolitan.

But there seem to be no records of any early Yorkshire immigrants lingering in New York. They had visions of a future not only in the mining trade, which they knew so well, but also in the farming of land on which they could settle and really call their own. Most set out to reach the Middle West, to the lead bearing limestone area and to the undeveloped farming lands of the Upper Mississippi Valley. But finding a way over vast distances of American territory to reach their destination called for both ingenuity and courage. From New York there were two main routes which these settlers seem to have followed. Many of the earlier Yorkshiremen are known to have travelled a distance of 100 miles to Philadelphia, a city regarded as a gateway over the Allegheny Mountains to Pittsburgh, Cincinnati and the Mississippi. Laid out by the Quaker William Penn as the capital of

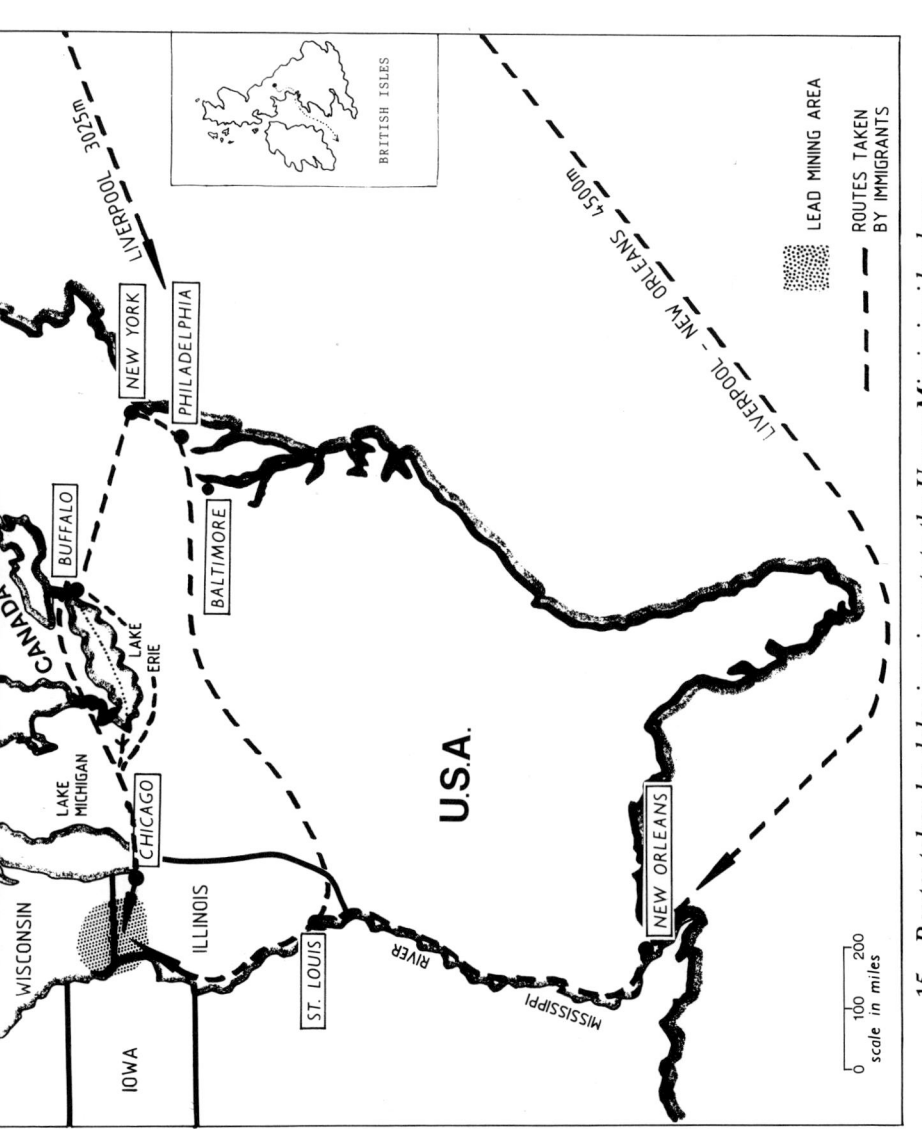

15 *Routes taken by dales immigrants to the Upper Mississippi lead area.*

Pennsylvania, Philadelphia had become a wealthy commercial centre. It had a population of 40,000 by 1775, larger at that time than New York and one of the biggest cities in the British Empire from which it was soon to secede.

Although the steam engine was a British invention, the speed and completeness of its application to North American conditions was quite extraordinary and a major factor in the country's development. As early as 1834, only 10 years after the original Darlington to Stockton passenger train in England, Philadelphia was linked with New York by the Camden and Amboy railroad. Progress was swift but American railroads were not generally created to connect important cities; rather, they were intended to provide access to individual centres from the surrounding country. The first locomotives were purchased from the Stephenson works in England, and even rails were imported during the early era of American railways. Although the New World lagged behind Britain in applying steam to ocean-going shipping, America was in the forefront in developing paddle-wheel steamboats, which were put into very effective use for river and canal transport. In these early days canals proved to be invaluable to the development of the economy, as they provided a much needed link between the natural waterways.

For the immigrants the route to Pittsburgh followed the Schuylkill Canal, the first section being 108 miles in length and reaching a point near the eastern Pennsylvania town of Pottsville. When Metcalf Bell and his wife left Gunnerside with a group of Swaledale emigrants in 1830, they recorded that, having travelled to Philadelphia from New York, it took them a further six days to reach Pottsville. There Metcalf Bell found work in the Schuylkill coal mines, as did three companions from Gunnerside, Henry and Anthony Hunt and John Holmes. Letters written at the time told of earnings amounting to $1.00 a day for work on a coal seam eight feet thick. Henry Hunt and his wife were to settle in the area and took a farm of 134 acres near Johnstown, on the route to Pittsburgh. But Metcalf Bell and his wife moved on through Pittsburgh and settled in Medina, Ohio.

James Pratt and his wife from Gunnerside also came to this area of Ohio though later they were to move to Dubuque, Iowa. Other dalesmen like Ambrose Hugill and Robert Waller, who arrived earlier, in 1828, are likely to have taken their route from Pittsburgh to Cincinnati and down the Ohio River to the Mississippi and St Louis. It was a formidable journey for these early settlers to follow the route to St Louis and the travel north to reach the lead-mining and farming areas of the Middle West. It was also a route favoured in part by Charles Dickens in 1842, when he made good use of paddle-wheel steamboats on his journey from Pittsburgh to the Mississippi River.

In 1825 the Erie Canal was opened. It was 363 miles long and linked the Great Lakes with the Hudson River and New York. Immigrants like William H. Calvert from Gunnerside in Swaledale and the group of dales people travelling with him to New York in 1839, chose to follow a route northwards to Buffalo and Lake Erie. They are likely to have used the steamboat service from New York for a journey of 150 miles up the Hudson River to Albany, then on to Buffalo by the canal. By then Buffalo had become a stopover between lake and canal traffic. Reports in these early times tell of bad conditions on canal passenger boats. Passengers they said were crowded like beasts into the available space, and exorbitant charges were frequent. Records indicate that William Calvert and his friends travelled on from Lake Erie and reached what was described as the 'village' of Chicago. Writing many years later about his journey, William Calvert said: 'In company with 17 young men we walked from Chicago to Galena (Illinois). Arrived just in time to celebrate the 4th July. Walked up to Council Hill same day and met with some English men. Then next day to New

Diggings (Wisconsin)'. From Chicago, their journey on foot carrying all their belongings must have been nearly 200 miles.

Only three years after William Calvert and his party made their journey, young William Coates, aged nine, travelled on a similar route with his parents from Swaledale, but they were shipwrecked on Lake Erie and lost all their belongings. Eventually they reached Dubuque, Iowa, where the family settled and found work in lead mining. In 1836 dalesman Joseph Brunskill and his wife are known to have followed a route to Cleveland, south of Lake Erie, and thence to Akron, Ohio. As described in a later chapter, the Brunskills were later to settle in Rockdale on Catfish Creek, south of Dubuque.

Even in the earliest days of the last century, and certainly by 1831, there were some immigrants from Yorkshire who made the long sea journey to New Orleans and then by steam packet boat up the Mississippi. The journey of about two months to the mouth of the river was followed by a further 1,300 miles of travel northwards by river steamboat. Early settlers from the dales seemed fascinated by the great width of the Mississippi, and they were concerned by their first sight of black slaves working in the Port of New Orleans. Letters written by the Yorkshire immigrants described New Orleans as a very unhealthy place with yellow fever and cholera common amongst the population. Certainly cholera was much feared, and when the Bonson family from Swaledale reached the Mississippi in 1834, Mrs Mary Spensley Bonson became a cholera victim and died during the journey. Her husband, Robert Bonson, and their son continued the journey and settled in Dubuque. A few years later Elizabeth Brunskill also died during the journey up the Mississippi, and her husband, Simon Brunskill from Gunnerside had to continue the journey to Dubuque with their three children. A similar fate befell Elizabeth Metcalfe, formerly Peacock, as she travelled up the Mississippi with her husband, Lister Washington Metcalfe.

Despite the long and sometimes hazardous journey, however, many more families from the Yorkshire Dales came to use this longer sea route from Liverpool, followed by steamboat travel to the lead mining area. But whatever the route taken by these immigrants, the majority were drawn as if by a magnet to the limestone area of the Middle West. In his study 'The Settlement of the Lead Mining Region' John Le Roy Grindell refers to it as an unglaciated (driftless) area with a radius of some 40 miles, set partly in Wisconsin, Illinois and Iowa, well drained and with a network of cross streams leading into the Mississippi. The main centres in this area were Dubuque, on the west bank of the Mississippi, and Galena, which became established on the tributary, Fever River. It was an area of rich lead bearing limestone, where there was not only mining work but the likelihood that good farming land would become available for those who wished to settle. There the men and women from the Yorkshire Dales could see a future for themselves and for their children. Somehow, the mining country along the banks of the Fever River seemed strangely like the valley of the Swale and other dales back in England.

Until the 1820s however, this Upper Mississippi limestone area had been exclusively the hunting ground of the American Indians, the Sauk, Mesquakie and Winnebago tribes, and even when the first of the Yorkshire immigrants arrived, it was by no means a settled area. There was much blood to be shed before the final exclusion of the Indians in 1832, and it was a sad period in their history.

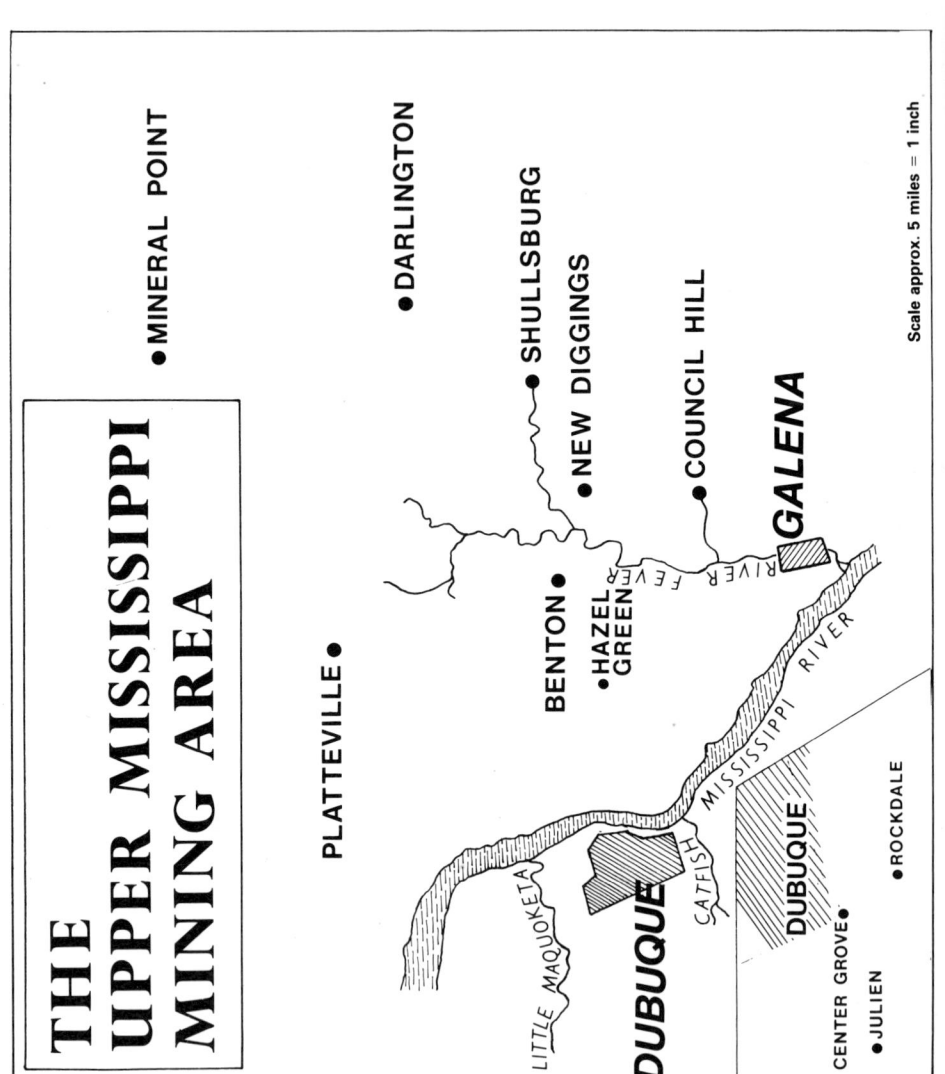

THE
UPPER MISSISSIPPI
MINING AREA

Scale approx. 5 miles = 1 inch

●MINERAL POINT

●DARLINGTON

●SHULLSBURG

●NEW DIGGINGS

●COUNCIL HILL

GALENA

BENTON●

●HAZEL GREEN

FEVER RIVER

PLATTEVILLE●

LITTLE MAQUOKETA

DUBUQUE

CATFISH

MISSISSIPPI RIVER

DUBUQUE

CENTER GROVE●

●JULIEN

●ROCKDALE

CHAPTER XI

Who are the Americans?

NORTH AMERICA HAS SOMETIMES BEEN referred to as a nation of immigrants. Certainly the United States as we know the country today embraces people of many lands making up a cosmopolitan society. But who were the Americans of earlier times? And was it really a land of promise to which the travellers from distant Yorkshire made their way? Before we continue with this account of the dales immigrants, let us look briefly at the vibrant history of North America and try to determine the origins of the American people.

When Christopher Columbus discovered America, he found natives which he called Indians. In fact, he might have been nearer the truth to call them Mongolians. 25,000 years or more ago, we are told, the forebears of those referred to as Indians were immigrants who had come from Asia via Siberia and reached the Seward Peninsula of Alaska. They stayed, finding ample supplies of fish and seal meat and as they gradually moved southward, they came to the warmer fertile land of plenty provided by the vast American continent. For a further 30,000 years or more they were left to expand and develop without intrusion, increasing in numbers and gradually forming an indigenous population which became dispersed over an area as far south as Patagonia. It was not until the arrival of Columbus and the Spaniards on the American mainland in 1498 that the European whites appeared on the scene. By then the Indians had developed their own advanced way of life, though their considerable numbers were mainly divided on a tribal basis. It was in fact their lack of unity which lead to their ultimate downfall.

Columbus was without doubt the effective European discoverer of the American continent, although it is recorded that Norsemen visited Newfoundland as early as the 11th century without making any permanent settlement there or on the mainland. The Spanish who came with Columbus and others who followed were seekers of gold and other treasures. This lure of gold and other treasures drew them mainly to the south, and by the beginning of the 17th century almost the whole of South America was in Spanish hands. Strangely enough, the very word 'America' appears to have originated from the first name of a Florentine merchant who sailed with the Spanish on a voyage to South America in 1499. He was Amerigo Vespucci and when he later wrote an account of his voyage, he gained such popularity that a German geographer suggested that the new continent be called after him.

By the end of the 16th century, with Elizabeth I on the throne of England, there was an urge by adventurers like Martin Frobisher, Sir Humphrey Gilbert and Sir Walter Raleigh to discover and to colonise. But it was not until the end of their war with Spain that, with sufficient funds then at their disposal, the English began to spread their colonies along the Atlantic coast of North America.

In the year 1620 a band of humble Pilgrims from East Anglia, after spending over 10 years in Holland, set out from Plymouth to cross the Atlantic in the 'Mayflower'. They landed on the southeast coast of what is today Massachusetts, and despite years of extreme hardship and near starvation, they established their settlement, Plymouth Colony. All agreed to be governed by the will of the majority until permanent provision could be made for their colony. This Mayflower Compact, as it has been called, and a system of government by a representative assembly adopted in Virginia, were the two foundation stones of subsequent American administration.

In Maryland, another colony was established that owed much to the initiative of a man with Yorkshire and particularly Swaledale connections. He was Sir George Calvert, and he became the first Lord Baltimore. For many centuries there have been Calverts living in the Swaledale area, though few appear to have been directly related to Sir George. Nevertheless, Lord Baltimore was born at Kiplin, close to the banks of the River Swale and within a few miles of Richmond. His career led him to the Court of James I and he was knighted in 1617. But in 1625 he resigned his office, reaffirmed his Catholic faith, and after attempts to set up a colony in Newfoundland, he sought and was granted land far to the south in Chesapeake Bay. But Lord Baltimore was to die before the Maryland Charter was issued and it was then taken up by his son Cecilius Calvert. The second Lord Baltimore proved to be a competent administrator, and he dispatched a group of 200 settlers to Maryland in 1634, arranged for his brother Leonard to be governor, established religious tolerance and devolved legislative procedures. Cecilius had intended that Maryland should not only thrive but also be a refuge for English and Irish Roman Catholics. In fact the colony eventually developed with a Protestant majority.

Another important colony was Pennsylvania, founded by the great Quaker William Penn. He regarded the colony as his 'Holy Experiment', and he attracted Quaker settlers from England and Wales and migrants from Germany – the Mennonites. They joined a small group of Swedes, Finns and Dutch settlers who had already found refuge in the area. Penn laid out his colony between the Delaware and Schuylkill Rivers and he promised religious and political freedom and easily acquired farm land. He was no businessman and encountered many problems, but his generous nature and charm helped to make Pennsylvania prosper. It was a portent of America as it was to become, the first large community in modern history where different races and religions could live under the same government on terms of equality. William Penn's idealism indeed brought success, as it did for Swaledale born Lord Baltimore and his son Cecilius Calvert.

By 1732 13 colonies had been established down the eastern coastal area, the last being Georgia, which became something of a buffer state against the Spanish in Florida. In 1735 Georgia was visited by the English missionary John Wesley, who later did much to establish the Methodist Church and visited the Yorkshire Dales on more than one occasion. He and his brother Charles stayed in Georgia only a few years before returning to England rather disillusioned. It seems that they found little scope for missionary work in what at that time was the weakest and least populous of the 13 colonies.

As a background to these east coast colonial territories there were the Appalachian Mountains and beyond, to the west, the territories of the Indians and the great Mississippi River. The Spanish held most of South and Central America as well as California and Texas and other territory to the west of the Mississippi River. To the north was Canada, where the French were located. With an eye to future trade and, no doubt, possible co-operation against the English, they took steps to build up an amicable relationship with the American Indians. The question was who would ultimately take control over Western North America. It was clearly a situation that would not be resolved without bloodshed.

Firstly, the threatened war between France and England burst into life lasting for seven years and being settled finally with a treaty signed in Paris in 1763. From this the English stood to gain all lands east of the Mississippi River, as well as French Canada and the best of the islands in the West Indies. But there was an increasing mood of independence amongst the established colonies. The settlers felt strongly that they should not be taxed without proper representation and when the English Parliament passed what was known as the Stamp Act, the opinion was that this single stroke lost Great Britain the affection of all her colonies. Tension built up, and the gap between war and peace began to vanish. The now historic Boston Tea Party and the dumping of tea from ships in Boston Harbour were followed by an incident at Concord in 1775 when British redcoats opened fire on a group of local citizens. It was the start of the American Revolution, an extraordinary war which lasted until 1783 and in which the Americans, mostly English immigrants fought troops of the Mother Country. Surprisingly, perhaps, it was the American colonies with a little help from the French and Spanish, who finally claimed victory. With this victory came independence and the birth of a new nation, which soon began to discover its identity.

A framework had now to be worked out for the efficient government of this new nation. To the credit of a younger generation of American politicians, as well as elder statesmen like Washington and Franklin, a Constitution was finally agreed upon and ratified. When the time came to elect the first President of the United States the unanimous choice was George Washington.

But America was not finished with wars. She still retained ties with France, so when war developed between France and Britain she found it impossible to remain neutral. Thomas Jefferson was then President, and though he tried to avoid involvement, America in the end found that she was at war with Britain. It lasted two and a half years and it was perhaps the most unnecessary war in history, reflecting little credit on the British, who learned at last that war with the United States was not worthwhile. In their efforts to invade the American east coast, the British burnt down public buildings in Washington, D.C., including the presidential mansion. It was later to be restored and painted white, and the White House in Washington stands today as a reminder of the independence and importance of the United States of America.

It was in the closing years of the 18th century and into the 19th that Americans ceased to look seaward as those in the eastern states had done for so long. They turned to the west, to the vast unexplored wilderness of the interior and to country extending even as far as the Pacific Ocean. The population was increasing and, by 1760 it reached over 1½ million. By 1820, there were 22 states and a population of nearly 10 million. This extraordinary build-up was due in part to large families and in part to immigration from Europe.

When the early settlers arrived in the New World from the Yorkshire Dales in the first half of the last century, the American people were of English, Welsh, Irish and Scottish stock, descendants of earlier settlers or recent immigrants. But there were also numbers of Germans and other Europeans, including some French Protestants. While these groups formed the core of the white population, there was also the very considerable number of African slaves, regarded by the white population of the southern states as an essential labour force. It was slavery which was to become a major issue between the northern and southern states, an issue which culminated in the terrible Civil War (1861-65).

But America was now a nation, and its peoples were increasingly conscious of their identity. During the later periods of the last century there was an escalation of immigration from European countries and the population continued to grow. But by then the pioneers from Yorkshire had long since made their mark in the areas we now know as Wisconsin, Illinois and Iowa, and they had been joined by many others from Swaledale and other dales. They had become part of a formidable nation of immigrants and of a vast and rapidly developing country.

CHAPTER XII

The Removal of the Indians

IT IS NOT EASY TO ESTIMATE the population of American Indians before the arrival of the Europeans, but there must have been over 10 million. They were the sole inhabitants of a continent rich in natural resources. Yet because they were thought to be backward by European standards, it has been said that the Indians needed to be discovered. Certainly, they welcomed the arrival of horses, goats and sheep, clothing and cooking utensils and particularly guns to replace their bows and arrows. What they did not welcome were the European diseases which could quickly spread through Indian families and cause much suffering if not death. But probably the introduction of intoxicating liquor, known as firewater, into the lives of the Indians was the white man's cardinal sin.

It was difficult for the Indians to understand the European conception of land ownership and the white man's desire to have more and more land for his own use. The Indian logic was that the land belonged to everyone. They were essentially hunters, and without land in which they could freely operate, they could not exist. But the Europeans were ruthless in their hunger for exclusive ownership of land; again and again they found ways of making treaties resulting in the expulsion of Indians from areas which had always been their hunting grounds. It was no credit to the white man that he frequently practised deception and dishonesty. Alcohol was known to have been used as a means to persuade Indians to give up land, and all too often, illiterate Indians were induced to put their marks to documents which they did not understand and had no right to sign.

With the colonisation of the eastern coastal areas of North America, the Indians were contained in lands west of the Appalachians. In 1763, a Royal Proclamation drew a line from north to south and prevented the American settlers from moving westward into the Indian area. This Proclamation was bitterly resented by the settlers, and their intention to defy the regulations received support from no less than George Washington who said, 'Those seeking good lands in the west must find them and claim them without delay'. In the event, there was continued pressure on the Indians and a gradual erosion of their position.

In the years following Independence the American peoples grew in number, became wealthier and asserted their dominance over the country. The Indians were now regarded by many people as no more than a nuisance and a barrier to progress. In 1830 the Indian Removal Act was passed and resulting in 60,000 Indians being moved from lands they had always occupied, and which had previously been guaranteed to them by treaty, to new territory far across the Mississippi. This great removal is well remembered not only because of its scale but also because of the bad faith of those who initiated it. It is true that some Indians were allowed to stay, but they were the few more influential half-breeds with well developed farms. Most Indian tribes were too feeble to resist the removal and there was cruelty and much human suffering as families were forcibly uprooted and often stripped of almost all they possessed. As the great mass of Indian people began the trek to the west, disease took the lives of many old people and children; cholera and measles were widespread and some tribes suffered additional hardship because of the severe winter weather. It was indeed a callous and degrading episode in the history of a new nation.

But what of the Indians of the Upper Mississippi? The role of the Sauk, the Fox – more correctly referred to as the Mesquakie – and Winnebago tribes was important, for it was these Indians who originally discovered the lead and mined it as best they knew. About 1695 a Frenchman named Le Sueur seems to have been the first white man to report the existence of the lead, though he did not become involved in any mining. Throughout the 18th century the Indians continued surface mining over a wide area of the Upper Mississippi Valley. They were encouraged to mine by other French explorers like Nicolas Perrot and then Julien Dubuque; and it was Julien who, in 1788, obtained a permit from a council of the Indian tribes to dig lead in the area in which now stands the City of Dubuque. His claim was confirmed in 1796 by a grant from the Spanish king.

The existence of what some called 'the treasure house' of lead in the Upper Mississippi was now becoming more widely known, and it was not long before further developments were afoot. Prior to 1822, the Mesquakie Indians were particularly active in the Fever River area, mining extensively where there was surface lead available. However, they had entered into a treaty with the government that allowed a tract of land 15 miles square in the area to be used by white men for mining purposes. By 1816 a trader known as Colonel George Davenport had been shipping lead down the Mississippi to St Louis. Then came Colonel James Johnson, who took out a lease and, with protection from a military guard, began his own mining in this Fever River area. He employed white miners and black slaves and used the best tools and equipment available. It heralded the federal government's decision to open up the area for white settlement by acquiring from the Indians all land east of the Upper Mississippi.

By 1825 there were said to be 100 miners working in the Fever River area, and by the middle of the following year, over 450. In 1827 there was a surge of incomers, including miners from Missouri as well as many adventurers who had no intention to settle but were gripped with a lead hysteria and came to make their fortunes. The Indians were restless however, and contended that the white men had moved beyond the boundary agreed upon under treaty. Word was sent to the settlers to prepare for an attack whereupon some of the people fled back to the Fever River settlement of Galena. But the threatened attack did not take place so some of the settlers who had fled felt able to return.

In 1831 Black Hawk, the elderly Indian leader tried to retain his ancient tribal seat at the mouth of Rock River, Illinois. However, squatters encroached on his village, they enclosed the Indian cornfields and even dug up the graves of his ancestors. Black Hawk withdrew into Missouri territory with his followers but there, the tribe came near to starvation and they had to contend with the very hostile Sioux Indians. In the hope of harvesting food and finding a vacant prairie in which to plant a new crop of corn, Black Hawk decided to return to the west. The following spring he crossed the Mississippi River with 1,000 of his tribe including women and children. Unfortunately, the inexperienced and glory seeking Illinois Militia, with Abraham Lincoln commanding a Company, misinterpreted the situation. Shots were fired and what followed could only be described as a tragic disaster.

Black Hawk and his Sauk followers moved northwards into Michigan territory (Wisconsin), followed by several hundred regular troops with 2,000 militia searching for a group of Indians who were not sure themselves where they were. The climax came when the Indians reached the mouth of the Bad Axe River on the Mississippi. They tried to build rafts and canoes to cross to the west but they were overtaken by the Warrior, an armed steamboat, and by soldiers on the shore. The display of Black Hawk's white flag of surrender was greeted with mistrust or ignored and in the wanton massacre which followed, all but 40 of the 1,000 Sauk men, women and children were slaughtered. This sad episode in American history and a treaty of 21 September 1832, marked the end of much of the Indian presence in the Upper Mississippi mining area.

CHAPTER XIII

Julien Dubuque
and the Business of Mining

THE EXTRAORDINARY THING ABOUT THE Frenchman Julien
Dubuque was the way in which he was able to gain the confidence
of the native Sauk and Mesquakie Indians in the limestone area to
the west of the Mississippi and around the Fever River. He seems
to have followed in the tradition of an earlier French trader Nicolas
Perrot, by being able to cultivate an easy friendship with the Indian
people. Julien had come from Canada, where at that time, the
population was still concentrated along the 160 miles of the
St Lawrence from Quebec to Montreal. His forebears were from
Normandy and Gascony in France, and Julien, small in stature,
was a man of intelligence and considerable charm.

He arrived in the Indian territory in 1788 and lived and worked
with them for over 20 years. By the time he died, they had come to
regard him as one of their own. There had of course been French
explorers and traders like Perrot, who took much interest in the
Indian lead mining but did not stay for any length of time. Julien
had known of the rich lead-bearing area, the limestone strip
immediately to the west of the Mississippi on which the City of
Dubuque now stands. At that time the area came within the
jurisdiction of the Spanish government, so before he started
mining the lead, he felt it right not only to have the approval of the

Indians but also of the Spanish governor of Louisiana. This was arranged, and with Indian labour at his disposal, Dubuque's 'Mines of Spain' – as Julien tactfully called them – produced regular supplies of lead which he shipped in 'pirogues' down the Mississippi to St Louis.

Julien Dubuque soon extended his operations to the area of the Fever River. He was a man of remarkable energy, and over the years he built up a very successful business which may have brought him considerable wealth. After his death the Indians displayed no love for intruding white adventurers and refused to permit anyone to cross the Mississippi from the east. These Sauk and Mesquakie Indians continued mining in the Dubuque area and when the territory was ceded to the United States as part of the Louisiana Purchase, the area was placed under the direct supervision of the U.S. government. Moreover, a small army detachment was sent to Dubuque to protect the Indians, particularly from white mining intruders.

The Black Hawk War of 1832 left few Indians in the area east of the Mississippi River and soon, many groups of white miners waited eagerly for permisson to cross the river and to begin mining in Dubuque's Mines of Spain. Some men had already been to the area and had found mining land which they wished to claim, though they had not been allowed to remain in the area. On 1st June 1833, agreement with the Indians having been ratified, permission to mine was given and there was a rush of men to cross the river to begin digging. Amongst the hundreds of men who crossed the river were fortune-hunting, roving miners as well as immigrants who came intending not only to mine but to find farming land and to settle in what was regarded as a much-coveted region. Located claims were registered and leased by the federal government to those agreeing orally before one witness, to work them 'in a diligent and miner-like manner'. Smelters were bonded, and paid the government 6% of the price of the finished lead. The area became what has been described as 'a fragmented labour camp', spreading from Catfish Creek in the south to the Little Maquoketa River in the north. In these early days it was an area where vigilante justice and lynch law prevailed. However, a Superintendent of Mines was appointed, a democratic miners' association was set up and a code of mining practice was agreed upon.

The miners who crossed the Mississippi River in 1833 were interested in the lead and not in building a city. They were content to erect log cabins for shelter and even the few small supply stores were set up in very jerry-built structures. But gradually, communities began to gather round a main street, soon there were small townships like Julien and Rockdale and by 1834, Dubuque County began to take its permanent shape as part of the 'Black Horse Purchase'. The town of Dubuque was officially named in the same year and it was soon to develop both as a centre and a river-port. A proper brick courthouse was built and it is recorded that by the autumn of 1835, there were 25 dry goods stores, numerous groceries, four taverns, a jail and three churches. Though the initial rush of miners slowed down, and a number of earlier arrivals left disappointed, there were rich deposits of lead to be found in the area and the future of the mining communities in Dubuque County seemed as assured as it was proving to be in the Fever River area.

In the days of the Indians, reports indicated that the squaws and older men did the mining work, leaving the 'bucks' to do the smelting, though one author, John Bradby, has suggested that the squaws did the smelting. Lead was often visible at surface level and the land areas became pock-marked with Indian workings. The incoming white men found mining a fairly simple process. A man working on his own could dig the lead ore from surface out-croppings, and a team of two or three men could sink a shaft and dig down 30 or 40 feet, as necessary. It was not usual for lead to be mined much below 50 feet for, at lower levels, water problems were likely to arise. Galena limestone, which contained the lead was generally below a layer of clay and slate. Most of the lead deposits were found in crevices from a few inches to a few feet wide, often expanding into caves, and generally in an east-west direction. Lead bearing veins often ran parallel with each other and appeared in groups. But for the miners, success depended very much on a 'rich strike' and was largely a matter of luck. Trial diggings where veins were identified from surface evidence often proved to be successful.

When Joseph Schafer wrote about the Wisconsin lead region, he discussed the equipment used by the early miners. Shafts were dug with a width of four to five feet, and a windlass fixed upon posts was set firmly on either side of the shaft. A suitably strong rope of adequate length was set up and lowered down the shaft attached to a bucket or tub. By this means unwanted diggings could be brought to the surface, as could the mineral, which would be brought by wheelbarrow to the foot of the shaft. When necessary, the sides of the shaft would be timbered for safety and, in the tunnels below the surface, pillars of rock would be left at intervals to support the roof. For lighting the mines, candles were set in gobs of clay which would adhere to any part of the rock wall. For tools, the miners had only shovels, a pick, gad or crowbar, a hand drill and some blasting powder.

Earliest reports of Indian smelting methods suggest that they did little more than throw their ore into the centre of a log fire. Probably through the influence of French traders, the Indians began to develop hopper-like excavations which were dug into a hillside and, with a base of stones to act as a grate and a covering of dry wood, it was possible to smelt a modicum of lead. Apparently the white miners continued to use this method at first with little improvement in the smelting process until an early form of hearth furnace came into use. This was certainly a more efficient method

17   *Cross-section of a lead mine from Plate IV of John C. Fremont's*
Report of the Exploring Expedition to the
Rocky Mountains (1845)

than the Indian smelting pits and it became possible to extract a higher proportion of the lead content in the ore. These furnaces were built of logs on hillsides in the form of three walls within which was the hearth and an 'eye' through which the melted lead passed into a receptacle. Apart from the considerable amount of fuel which they used, the problem was that, at first, they were built with the local limestone and the heat generated by the log fire soon reduced the stone to lime. It was not until good firebrick could be used in the building of these furnaces that they had any length of life.

In the lead areas of the Upper Mississippi the miners came to realise how dependent they were on the smelting process – indeed,

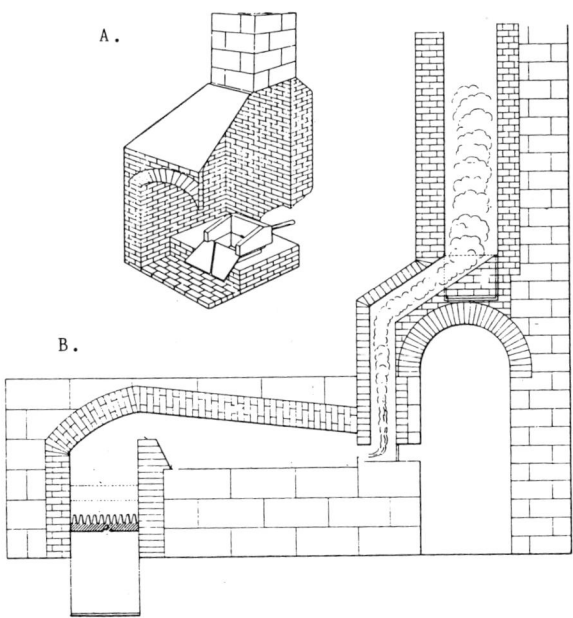

18   *Drawings of (a) the Scotch hearth lead smelting furnace as used at Dubuque (from the Iowa Geological Survey 10, 1899), and (b) a horizontal reverberatory furnace as developed in England.*

the smelting men were soon recognised as the most important and powerful in the industry. In seeking to improve the efficiency of the furnaces, the smelters had to overcome problems not unlike some already faced by mining folk in parts of Britain and in Germany and Spain. In England, the hearth smelting system had been developed in various forms over a period of several centuries with considerable success. In a lead area of Britain like Swaledale where there were a number of individual mining units and plenty of peat for fuel, hearth furnaces were generally favoured. A rewarding development in the American mines was the use of the blast-furnace system. Writing about this system, the American mining engineer M. Eissler noted that it produced the higher working temperature necessary for low-grade ores. The system used a refractory lining in the hearth and the blast was provided by mechanical blowers. Furnaces using this method of smelting had a 15 foot chimney.

An alternative smelting method developed was the horizontal reverberatory system*, which had found favour in England with larger mining concerns. This system which differed considerably from the ore hearth smelters, was brought into use in Britain by the middle of the 18th century, and was adapted by Robert Drummond for use in the Upper Mississippi lead region. However, the ore hearth smelting furnaces were the more adaptable as far as fuel was concerned. Their efficiency continued to improve and they were ideal for areas with many small mining units. The reverberatory smelters were costly to build and demanded higher fuel quality, but they were otherwise very

---

* The horizontal reverberatory furnaces developed in England were known to be about ten feet long and two feet high in the centre. The flame was obtained from a fire usually of coal sited at one end of the smelter and the flames, hot air and gasses were drawn over a low fire bridge to bear upon the ore in the bed of the furnace, the draught being created by a tall chimney. This type of furnace was sometimes used for roasting, a preliminary smelting process intended to dissipate the sulphur and antimony contained in the ore.

efficient and had a larger capacity for continuous working. Though their basic functions remained the same, these different smelting systems were often subjected to modifications in design wherever they were erected.

Once the Fever River area, and later Dubuque, was opened to white men, there was a concentrated and rapid development of mining operations. Though digging out surface lead in the early days was mainly a labouring job for the hundreds of men who appeared to stake their claims, only a few had any experience with smelting. While those who began to smelt had often to improvise, developments were clearly based on the methods used in Europe. Men with any prior knowledge or with recent experience, like some from the dales of Yorkshire, had an invaluable head start. But they needed to adapt to local conditions; whereas in Yorkshire there was peat and some coal to be had, wood was the only fuel available to the Upper Mississippi smelters. Logs and charcoal had therefore to provide the furnace heat required. This was quite adequate for the ore hearth smelters but local wood supplies were not unlimited. Coal and coke became available later, particularly when the railway system was developed. But such solid fuel was expensive and when the mining of zinc took precedence over lead, much of the zinc ore was sent away from places like Mineral Point, Wisconsin, for smelting in the coal-mining areas.

Clearly, there was always some doubt whether the efficient reverberatory smelters could be properly fuelled in the limestone lead-bearing area and whether they could really be adapted to mining by many small operators. Indeed, according to Joseph Schafer, most of the reverberatory furnaces that came to be built in the lead mining area of the Middle West eventually gave way to improved ore hearth smelters, particularly the so-called Scotch hearth blast furnaces.

CHAPTER XIV

The Development of Dubuque

THE 'GOLDEN AGE' OF LEAD MINING in the Dubuque area was from 1835 to 1849 although mining continued in a diminished way for many years. Amongst the early settlers who crossed the Mississippi and found their way mainly to the west and south of what is now Dubuque were a number from the Yorkshire Dales. Names like Bell, Bonson, Brunskill, Coates, Daykin, Kilburn, Pratt, Waller and Watters are only some that came to be known in the area. These were people born and bred into a world of lead mining. They had much to contribute and some played important roles in developing improved mining and smelting processes.

Amongst these early immigrants from the Yorkshire Dales, there are those who deserve particular mention. Joseph Brunskill, for instance, came to America in 1833 with his wife, formerly Elizabeth Woodward. After working as a wood chopper and labourer in Cleveland, Ohio for three years, he and his family moved to Dubuque. He worked as a miner for a while and then took a partner and in 1845 built a smelter at Rockdale near Dubuque. This developed into an extensive business, and when he retired in 1871, he was acknowledged as a man whose ability and excellent judgment had done much to promote the prosperity of the Dubuque area.

Much is known of the Bonson family who came to Dubuque from Swaledale in 1834. Robert Bonson arrived with his 19 year

19, 20   *Richard Bonson and Harriett Watts Bonson.*

21   *The Bonson home in Dubuque, Iowa.*

old son Richard but, as mentioned earlier, his wife Mary Clarkson Bonson, had died of cholera near St Louis during the journey up the Mississippi. With the Bonsons came Richard Waller from Whitaside in Swaledale, with his wife formerly Mary Harker, and their four children. Richard Waller, an experienced smelter, with his brother Robert and with Richard Bonson, erected a blast furnace on a site at Platteville, Wisconsin. It was said to be the first blast furnace for smelting lead ever built in the United States. In the same year they erected two more, one of which was sited at Big Patch southwest of Platteville. With a group of other interested people, they formed a company to build furnaces, but this proved to be too cumbersome so smaller companies like Waller & Co of Catfish were later to be formed. Richard Bonson lived on for some 50 years in Dubuque County and, by the time of his death in 1883, he had not only made his mark in the mining industry, he had been elected to the state legislature and filled a number of other responsible positions, including the State Inspector of Banks.

Another immigrant lead smelter was John Watters, who came from Gunnerside in Swaledale. He was responsible for building a smelting furnace north-west of Rockdale and this Watters family smelter continued to operate through three generations of the family. It was said to be the last furnace to remain in operation in the Dubuque area. Another Swaledale man noted in the records is George Reynoldson, who operated a smelter at Center Grove and also a tanning yard and later, a leather business in Dubuque.

Most incomers from the Yorkshire Dales had been brought up as men of the land as well as miners. One outstanding example was James Pratt, who came to America from Gunnerside in 1833 with his wife, formerly Hannah Coates. They found their way to Akron in the Medina County, Ohio and for two years, they cleared 50 acres of heavily timbered land to set up a farm. But James had seen a newspaper article describing the lead mining in the Upper Mississippi region and, leaving his wife to keep the farm, he set out

22   *The Watters family smelter at Rockdale.*

to walk the 500 miles to Dubuque. He swam rivers, waded creeks and slept on the ground at nights. He ate in houses when he could and killed game when he was hungry. When he arrived, he worked in the mines for a time and then found his way back to his Ohio farm. He stayed on the farm for two years and then decided to sell it and return to Dubuque with his wife. There he joined with two others in buying Catfish Mill, which was used for 'cracking corn'. This venture was so successful that a larger mill was soon built and also prospered. In turn, this was replaced by a stone structure known as the Rockdale Mills. By the time he died in 1869, James Pratt was regarded as a greatly respected citizen; he was a director of three banks, and his obituary referred to him as one of the founders of Dubuque, one of the oldest of the old settlers and 'one of the noblest of them all'.

It is interesting to recount the experiences of David and Ralph Fawcett, who arrived in America from Swaledale and decided that they must go to the California goldfields. They are said to have bought an old bullock and a wagon and trekked across the plains to the West. On reaching California, they must have made money in gold mining, for they journeyed back a few years later to reach West Dubuque. After acquiring several farms, they married and settled down to live to the ripe ages of 84 and 86, respectively. They left a number of descendants.

By the 1840s Dubuque had begun to lose its image as a large mining camp and a new generation of buildings began to appear. Though at first it was a fragmented city it was to develop into a compact and important centre. Immigration brought in considerable numbers of European families, and by 1860 it was said that the majority of Dubuquers had been born in other countries, mostly in Ireland and Germany. The English, including those who had come from the Yorkshire Dales, tended to live in the hinterland to the south and west and some on the 'bluffs' above Dubuque.

The economy of Dubuque had been founded on the lead mining but it was soon to be boosted by a considerable timber trade and a meat packing industry. Before long it was the largest employer of factory workers in Iowa and during the years between the American Civil War and the first World War, it continued to develop and become a prosperous city. Many years have now passed since its foundation and even a man with the vision of Julien Dubuque could hardly have envisaged a city bearing his name to be built in the area of 'The Mines of Spain'.

In 1876 James Lonsdale Broderick left his home in Swaledale to visit America, and especially to go to the Dubuque area. Like his father before him he kept a diary which told of his meetings with the many dales people who had settled there. Some 40 years had passed since the arrival of the earliest settlers but some were still there to greet him as were their sons and daughters and a new generation all linked by history with the far off Yorkshire Dales. James Broderick died soon after his return to England but his diary continues to remind us of the Dubuque of earlier years and of the important role played by the pioneering dalesmen.

CHAPTER XV

Galena and the Fever River Miners

To ask why the Fever River was given its name is to invite a variety of answers. Perhaps it was derived from the French La rivière aux fèves, which originated from the quantity of 'fève' or bean flowers along the river bank. Or maybe the river was named after an early French trader known as La Fèvre. Whatever the true answer, the river as seen today seems no more likely to have been a health hazard – a source of fever – than the Mississippi itself. What is certain is that the River Fever, later to be renamed the Galena River, came to play a vital role in the development of mining in the limestone area east of the Upper Mississippi.

At the head of the Fever River, seven miles from its junction with the Mississippi is Galena which was given its name in 1826. In the early 1820s, it was just a small settlement, and had been referred to as La Pointe or January's Point. But by 1822 when the first steamboat came up the River Fever the settlement was beginning to develop in importance. Soon a group of 43 settlers under the leadership of a Dr Moses Meeker arrived and, at that time, the 100 or more mining folk already there were reported to be 'living in caves in the rocks'. Moses Meeker and his party moved up the River and struck lead at Hardscrabble near Hazel Green. In 1824, a store was opened in the Fever River settlement to provide supplies for the rapidly increasing influx of miners and

23, 24   *Galena depicted in its early days as a settlement, and in later years as an important river port and trading centre.*

adventurers. Having been given the name of Galena, the settlement was soon to grow into a commercial centre. It became important as a port, a lead market and a base for supplies. Though its role was an entrepôt for the district, the very nature of the lead industry tended to promote an unstable population. Despite the speed of its early development, the City of Galena did not increase greatly in size in later years. Today it has retained much of its history and it is an attractive centre with its houses built into the hillside on either side of the river.

It was but a mile up the Fever River from the site of Galena that, as early as 1819, the Sauk and Mesquakie Indians who were mining in that area, raised what history describes as an 'enormous nugget' of lead. The Indians were members of a group called 'The Buck', and there is little doubt that their mine was extremely rich in lead. Word of such a find and of great mining possibilities in the area, soon attracted attention. By 1823 nine leases had been granted to prospecting miners but soon many more newcomers arrived. Described as squatters, prospectors and fortune hunters, they paid little attention to leasing enactments made by Congress.

Most of these incomers came up-river to Galena and then followed the course of the Fever in their search for lead. In a number of areas they found traces of earlier Indian mining, the 'old diggings' as they were called, and these sometimes guided the incomers to profitable beds of ore. As another guide, some prospectors looked for what they called 'the masonic weed', possibly the Amorpha Canescens, a bush thought to be 'rooted in lead'. Probably the first mining settlement, sited to the north and close to the Fever River, was given the name Natchez. It was there that, some while later, James Harker from Swaledale built a house which was afterwards taken over by another dalesman, David Fawcett. Though the settlement of Natchez now exists only in history, the name of the village of New Diggings sited nearby in 1824, is still with us today. It is a name originally applied to an area in which the first prospectors found many traces of earlier Indian workings. This area proved to be rich in lead and many new finds were uncovered especially on land which the miners called New Diggings Ridge. Into this mining area came a number of immigrants from the Yorkshire Dales. Some went to what became known as English Hollow to the south of New Diggings. Later, others appear to have lived nearby in Richmond, a settlement sited on the banks of the Fever River. There, a smelter was built for extracting lead and zinc and no doubt the Swaledale emigrants who went to the settlement named it after the Richmond they had known by the River Swale in England.

As more 'nomad miners' and other men moved into the area there was a 'free-for-all' approach to prospecting, so it is not surprising that arguments and sometimes violence arose as men disputed the right to work a particularly rich find. The new arrivals wasted little time before starting to dig. Housing was of no concern and, so intent were some of the newcomers to make money that they lived as 'badgers' in dens or caves on the hillsides or in hastily constructed log shelters. In time, further settlements were set up like Council Hill, Illinois, Shullsburg, and Hazel Green, Wisconsin. The miners sometimes smelted small quantities of ore themselves, but generally they needed to go to a licensed smelter. From the smelting furnaces, teams of oxen or mules, and later horses, hauled the ore to Galena where it was sent down to the Mississippi and St Louis, using flatboats.

In 1827 miners began collecting at Mineral Point, which was further to the north and on land still owned by the Winnebago Indians. The settlement took its name from a nearby hill or extension of the prairie and it began in the shape of two log huts erected in 1827 by a Baptist minister Elder William Roberts and two companions. The American Henry Dodge then arrived with his family and some slaves. He erected a stockade a few miles to the north and began mining and log smelting. News of successful

25, 26   *Two examples of log houses built by early immigrant miners,*
(a) a log hut built into the hillside, and
(b) a more permanent log homestead in which a miner and his
wife lived with their ten children.

strikes in the vicinity soon attracted miners, merchants and speculators. Crude huts were built, and gradually Mineral Point became a town, a centre for the mining community to the north of the Fever River and later the county seat. In 1829 the first school was founded, and it is recorded that there were eight pupils taught by a Mrs Harker. She is thought to have been the wife of an early dales immigrant, one of several who found their way to the Mineral Point area in the late 1820s. They included John and Mary Spensley, who were later to join with James Calvert and others in forming the mining and smelting business of Spensley and Company.

To the south-west of Mineral Point is Platteville which was founded by a Kentucky Methodist James Hawkins Rountree, who arrived in the lead area about 1827. It was to become an important mining centre and, as already mentioned, it was at Platteville that Richard Waller and his companions from Swaledale built the first blast furnace. A number of other dales people became established in the Platteville area, including the Hugills of which Thomas Hugill was probably the earliest. He is known to have worked for Major Rountree in surveying the Platteville site and is later recorded as being appointed Assessor for the town. By 1850 there were about 90 English families living in or around the town. But in time, the population became very cosmopolitan. As it developed, Platteville was not only a mining town but also a centre for secondary education. An academy was established and it became a focal point for advanced education in the area.

As the mining population increased, the government planned to retain contol over mineral land by requiring each miner to pay over the equivalent of one tenth of the lead he produced. As R. W. Chandler recorded when he published the first detailed map of the lead area, a lot of 200 yards square was allowed to every two miners and it was stipulated that mineral mined must be sold to a licensed smelter. But those miners who had moved north into what was still regarded as Indian land claimed that they were paying a rent to the Winnebagos and that therefore, no money should be payable to the government. Uncertainty and anger developed amongst the men, and they petitioned the government for all land to be put up for sale. But it was some years before they had their wish fulfilled.

By the middle of 1829 it became clear that a recession which had already troubled Eastern America had now reached the Upper Mississippi and the mining area. Lead prices fell substantially and the recession resulted in food becoming scarce and expensive. It was said that a miner had to produce four to five thousand pounds of lead in order to buy a barrel of flour. As living conditions deteriorated and as fears grew of an attack from the Winnebagos, many miners abandoned their claims. Some moved into farming but there were others who began to leave and seek their fortune elsewhere. The hard times continued throughout 1830 and into the following year. In the spring of 1832 Black Hawk and his band of Sauks crossed the Mississippi River from the west and headed northwards. It was thought that they would link up with the Winnebago Indians in an effort to regain their former territory. Though this did not happen, there was alarm and uncertainty and many more miners and their families hurriedly left the area and journeyed southwards to Galena. However, the Black Hawk War as it came to be called, was short lived and, by the 'fall', calm had been restored. But by then, hundreds had left the mining country never to return.

Those who had remained during the Black Hawk scare were soon to be re-joined by some who had gone to Galena and now decided to re-trace their steps. A new land survey was instigated, and by 1833 the door was open to new immigrant settlers who could not only mine but could farm and develop the agricultural potential of the land. Sadly, as an aftermath of the Black Hawk War, asiatic cholera broke out and caused considerable concern in the Fever River area. Yet future prospects improved with a rise in lead prices. In 1834, a Land Office was opened in Mineral Point and anyone who had occupied and cultivated any part of a quarter section during the previous year could purchase the land at $1.25 an acre, provided the land was not ore-bearing. Wood was essential to the economy and, as local supplies were already showing signs of running down, any timber land was regarded with special importance. But the separation of mineral and non-mineral land caused many problems and, in the end, a sort of owner farmer – mineral tenant system had to be evolved. It was 1847 before it became possible to purchase mineral rights.

CHAPTER XVI

The Settlers from the Dales

WHEN THE LAND OFFICE OPENED IN Mineral Point it was the early settlers in this Upper Mississippi lead region who were to be the most favoured in the way of land selection. Of those who remained during and after the Black Hawk War of 1832 there was a hard core of American born men who in their various ways were outstanding in the history of those times. Henry Dodge, William Field, Henry Gratiot and Robert Champion are but a few of the well remembered names. Amongst the immigrants, there were numbers of Irish but there were also men like Ambrose Hugill and Robert Waller from the Yorkshire Dales. Others were to arrive from the dales later in the 1830s; men with names like Alderson, Atkinson, Daykin, Kilburn, Raw, Spensley and Woodward. When the teacher and historian Margaret B. Carter listed the first English immigrants to New Diggings area, she included John Redfearn, Thomas Peacock, Martin, Michael and Isiah Calvert, Amos and Simon Harker, Joseph Sedgewick, David Fawcett, Christopher Wiseman, and William Pedley all of whom came from Swaledale or from the dales nearby. Many of these immigrants lived in 'English Hollow' to the south of New Diggings.

It is perhaps not surprising that the balance of the growing population at that time suffered because of the small number of females. When Jonathan Alderson, an immigrant from

Arkengarthdale, wrote home from New Diggings to his relatives in England, he said 'I recommend any young man who comes to bring a wife. Of three hundred miners, half are bachelors.' Jonathan gave some revealing impressions of life in the mining area; '. . . the only faults are the wickedness of the people. You would find it impossible to utter the oaths that an American has in his regular discourse'. But he was impressed by the lack of hierarchical structure in American frontier life. 'We have no crown' he wrote, 'no duty, no bishops, nor yet have I seen a beggar running from door to door nor anything like an overseer gathering rates. We sit in our humble little cot free of rent, we can turn on the prairie horses or cows free and, by humbly asking leave to mow, we can have as much hay as we please. No gamekeepers, we work as we please, we play when we please, we have no Stuarts to bow to, one is as independant as another but we never forget our native land.'

William H. Calvert was one of the immigrants who returned to Swaledale to find a wife. He had been in the Fever River area for 10 years and by 1848 he would have become well established in his new country. Back in the hills of Swaledale he married Jane Alton in the church at Muker and he and his bride sailed in the ship 'Saxony' from Liverpool in 1849 bound for New Orleans and then by steamboat up the Mississippi. They settled to live a happy and successful life in Benton, where they remained for over 50 years. William Calvert farmed and mined and dealt in real estate. He did much for Benton, helping in the development of its first school and the Methodist Church. When he died, his obituary referred to him as a highly esteemed citizen and a pioneer resident of Benton. He was survived by nine children and the family name is continued in the Benton of today.

William Calvert had arrived as a new immigrant in 1839 at a time when America, and the Eastern States in particular, was beginning to recover from a worrying period of inflation. After the removal of the Indians, land sales and a quickly developing economy had

27, 28   *William Harker Calvert and his wife Jane.*

brought increased wages and prices. There was speculation and borrowing, too much paper money came into circulation and President Jackson became alarmed with the situation as it developed. Though the miners and the farmers of the Upper Mississippi seemed to escape the worst of these hard times many traders and other businesses are known to have suffered. But by 1840, inflation seemed to be in control and there was a gradual upturn in the economy. It was during the 10 years which followed that the numbers of immigrants really began to increase.

Passenger lists of American vessels crossing the Atlantic during that period confirm the numbers of dales people who emigrated and found their way to the Upper Mississippi area, most to join relatives and friends who had made the journey in earlier years. Many more came from Swaledale but there were others from

Wensleydale and Wharfedale. From adjoining dales to the north, there were mining men from Teesdale and Weardale and some came from Northumberland. A close bond remained between these mining families but they gradually became integrated over a wide area of the mining and farming country.

Much has been written about the Cornish tin miners who came to the Upper Mississippi area, driven from the mines of Cornwall by low wages and generally hard times in their homeland. They had begun coming by the 1830s and their numbers increased considerably in subsequent years. With their deep mining experience they soon found work in the lead area. But they were a distinctive 'ethnic' group and, rather than disperse throughout the area, they tended to congregate in places like Mineral Point. They drew attention because of their distinctive names, customs and dialect and their contribution to the character of the area is recorded in local history. Yet they found it difficult to assimilate compared with the Yorkshiremen whose nature and traditions allowed for rapid absorption into the American social order. Strangely enough there seems to be evidence that some immigrants from the Yorkshire Dales were recorded as having come from Cornwall. Comparatively few of the Cornishmen seemed to settle into long term lead mining and farming and by 1850, when California gold mining became an attraction, the Cornish immigration to this lead area was soon to cease.

In 1847 it became possible for claimant settlers and miners to purchase reserved lands. Many of these lands were already being used for both farming and mining but the purchase of the reserved mineral land gave a new feeling of permanence which had previously been lacking. Sales through the land office at Mineral Point in 1847 involved 117,500 acres, a figure which suggests considerable demand. The leasing system which the government had tried to operate with little success suddenly began to be effective. As the time approached for the reserved land sales, the

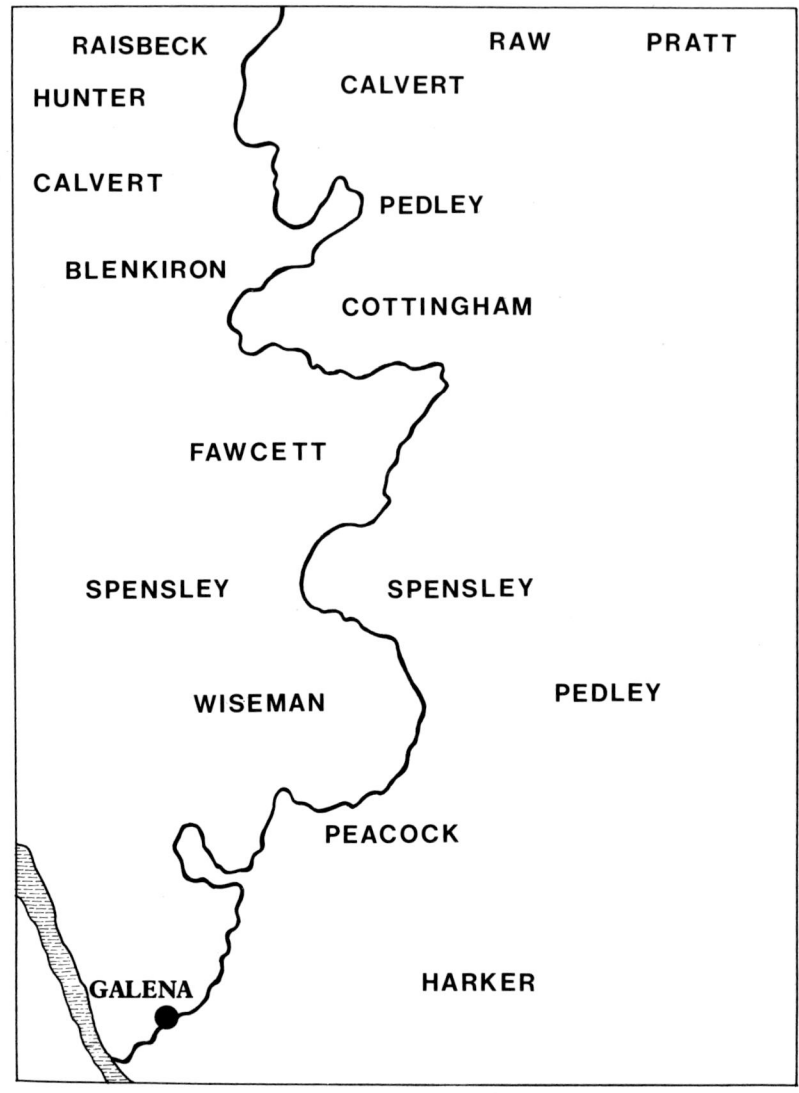

29 *A map of the Fever River with the names of some settlers from the Yorkshire Dales and the areas in which they developed their own land. Some holdings were small, others extensive, and though some family mining continued for many years, farming was to become the main occupation for these immigrant dales people.*

'squatters' who had mined and farmed on land without any legal authority found they needed proof of possession and they rushed to obtain a proper lease.

As already mentioned, the early arrivals in the region were the most favoured by being able to take the land of their choice after the Black Hawk War and later to buy whatever reserved land they had leased. Robert H. Champion and Frank Dering were two Americans who acquired some large areas around New Diggings and later decided to lease or rent-out pieces of their land. John Redfearn, for example, was a miner from the Yorkshire Dales who was able to lease and then to buy land from Champion and Dering. He established the firm of Redfearn and Company and he became a man of some wealth. When, in 1850, the California goldfields lured many men away from the area, the settled immigrants had more opportunity to buy up land which then became available.

Many early immigrants from the dales arrived in the Upper Mississippi area with very little money. It was not until they found work in the mines and saved their earnings that they could fulfil their great wish to have their own land. Many parcels of land contained lead, and when a map of the Benton and New Diggings area was produced later in the century, the considerable number of small mining units could clearly be seen. There were nearly 50 mines in the Benton area alone. Some were given odd names like Jug Handle, Jack of Diamonds or just Eureka! Others were named after the owners; there were mines named after Yorkshire immigrant families from the dales, like Calvert, Cottingham, Hird, Metcalf, Milner, Peacock, Pratt, Raisbeck, Spensley and Wiseman. History relates that, after its closure, the Raisbeck mine was reported to be used as a hideout by the notorious Dillinger Gang. Of the bigger mining units, the Robert Champion mines on the New Diggings Ridge probably provided the greatest yield of all. One section known as the Champion's 'old lode' was particularly lucrative; it was claimed to have been discovered by

30, 31   *The Champion Mine of yesterday and today.*

John Alderson, one of several Swaledale men believed to have worked in the Champion mines area.

With the arrival of an increasing number of immigrants into the area, the period 1840-50 proved to be a time not only of considerable mining and commercial activity but also for improvement and consolidation. The huts and shacks in which the early mining folk had made their homes were gradually replaced by wooden framed houses and, as business activity increased, there was a call for transport arrangements to be improved. In her description of those times, Margaret S. Carter referred to the many merchants who come to do business in New Diggings, the hotels, gambling houses and saloons, and the new farms and mines which were being opened up. This was also a time for the building of churches and schools. A Primitive Methodist church was built in New Diggings in 1846 and several Yorkshire Dales immigrants, including Isiah Gill and Thomas Robinson, were involved in its development. In Leadmine, William Pedley from Swaledale was one of the founders of the Methodist Episcopal church and

32 *A miners boarding house built at New Diggings.*

members of the local Primitive Methodist church included a number of dales families. A Leadmine school was built and dalesman Henry Clarkson was treasurer to the School Board. William Calvert did much to create a new school in Benton and there both Methodist and Catholic churches were later to be built, the Catholic church being one of several established in the lead area and inspired by a respected spiritual leader, Father Samuel Mazzuchelli.

With the building of better houses, churches and schools there was surely confidence of a settled and peaceful future. Yet 1861 saw the beginning of a disastrous period for the whole nation – the four years of the American Civil War.

33   *The Raisbeck Mine at Benton, Wisconsin.*

34   *Miners working at the E.M. & M. Mine (The Metcalf Mine).*

35   *The Calvert Mine at Benton, Wisconsin.*

36   *A group of miners including members of the Hunter, Blades, Harker and Hird families from the Yorkshire Dales.*

37 *Another group of miners including two Calverts and other dales immigrants.*

38 *A typical family smelter.*

CHAPTER XVII

The Civil War and the New Beginning

HAD SHE NOT WRITTEN Uncle Tom's Cabin, history might not have remembered Harriet Beecher Stowe. But her book was widely read at a time when slavery was creating mounting tension between the American South and the North. There is little doubt that Mrs Stowe's story did much to convince her readers, and especially those in the North, that slavery was indeed a hateful practice. Such was the impact made by the book that, in retrospect, Abraham Lincoln was said to observe 'Uncle Tom's Cabin was the cause of the American Civil War'.

The story of black slavery delves deep into American history. Many recognised it as an evil practice and such opinion led to the passing of a federal law in 1808 ending the importation of slaves from Africa. This meant that the Southern cotton planters needed to preserve and make better use of their existing slave population. Slavery meant power and prosperity to the planter class. The export of cotton to England was particularly lucrative and the planters rejoiced in the profits of their slave labour. Some planters were arrogant in their personal behaviour and to free their slaves was quite unthinkable. Yet underneath, many felt profoundly insecure and feared that, if given an opportunity, their slaves would rise up and seek horrible revenge. But the economic argument to continue slavery and avoid the dangers of black emancipation was strong enough to win continuing majority support in all the Southern states.

Tension between the North and South continued to develop, and there were many incidents in history which emphasised the fragile nature of the American Union. By 1860, Southern nationalism had developed to such an extent that state after Southern state began to secede from the Union and to form a new Confederated States of America. A presidential election was held and Abraham Lincoln won without carrying any of the Southern states. Though Lincoln's election was said to have triggered off the secession, the great divide between North and South had really only one root cause – and that was slavery.

The process of secession in the South was a body blow to the whole image of the Union of American States. The pride in the achievements of the American Revolution had been enormous, and the belief in liberty and equality was so profound that few in the North could comprehend the divisive situation that had developed. Abraham Lincoln was not to be sworn in as president until March 1861 and, in the meantime, the weak Buchanan remained as an ineffective president, quite unable to deal with the crisis. The Confederacy elected Jefferson Davis as its provisional president in February, and the Southern states were now joined together as a new nation 'seething with bombastic pride'.

When he came into office, Abraham Lincoln played for time, as he had no wish to fire the first shot, hoping as he did that armed conflict could still be avoided. But on 12th April, 1861 the Confederacy began bombarding Fort Sumter in Charleston harbour and a war began which was to last four long years and to result in the death of some 500,000 Americans. The military potential of the North, its large population and its command of the sea gave it an advantage which should have resulted in a speedy victory. But when war came, the abolitionists of slavery were divided and some welcomed the South's secession. Abraham

Lincoln was cautious and there was no wish for a long drawn-out conflict. In the South, the cotton production plummeted as exports by sea were blockaded. The slaves were unsettled and the military forces untrained. Yet the war dragged on, bitter battles developed and after two years, both sides had to resort to conscription. Casualties mounted and in the two day confrontation at Gettysburg it is said that both sides lost over 20,000 men. The death toll continued and it was not until the spring of 1865 that the forces of the Confederacy were finally overcome and slavery was outlawed for ever. Even when peace eventually came after this bloodiest conflict in American history it was marred by the assassination of the greatest leader of his time, President Abraham Lincoln.

By the time of the Civil War there had been a slowing down of immigration to the mining area of the Upper Mississippi. Of those who were settled in the area many were willing to serve in defence of the Union, and it was only the 'nomad' immigrants who objected strongly to the war and to being drafted into military service. Many Yorkshire immigrants are known to have served or to have been ready to play their part if required. William Blades, a Swaledale man, wrote later of his army service in the Civil War, and there are others known to have served but did not survive the conflict. In the New Diggings area, another dalesman, James Harker, was appointed Deputy Sheriff to help enrol all local able-bodied men. Those not required for more active service probably included older men and some were organised into a 'home guard'. The Lafayette Guard formed 'to maintain the authority of the law' was comprised very largely of men originating from the Yorkshire Dales.

It was in the early 1860s that demand increased lead prices and this was particularly important to the Champion Mine which had been carrying out much drainage work. A new 'strike' was so rich that it provided about seven million pounds of lead and furnished material for many of the bullets fired during the Civil War. But the days of the pioneer lead mining were coming to an end. The surface lead supplies were becoming exhausted and mining at a deeper level was more costly. When the war ultimately drew to its close, lead prices fell rapidly and lead mining ceased to bring the rewards of earlier years.

It was after the War that the mining of zinc became more profitable than lead. Though a number of lead mines continued to operate after the Civil War they gradually closed or gave way to the production of zinc. However, the mining of zinc needed more capital equipment and the facilities of concerns like the Wisconsin Zinc Company, who took over the Champion Mine. By 1882 zinc production far exceeded that of lead and the Mineral Point zinc mining area became particularly important. Demand continued to increase and the First World War brought a new boom in zinc trading. Despite a subsequent recession, demand revived during the War of the 1940s and zinc was still mined until 1947, when with the removal of government subsidies, the mines were faced with closure.

After the end of the Civil War and in the remaining years of the 19th century, the people of the mining areas began once more to build a settled future. There was a further influx of immigrants including a number from the dales, many being related or having close connection with earlier settlers. More land was developed for farming, railroads were extended and the people began to be more concerned with matters of government and in the way their towns and villages were administered. With the growth of communities, there were more shops, small businesses, new schools and churches. These were years of goodwill, there was time to socialise, for horse racing and other sports. Then came the present century, two world wars and times of both plenty and recession.

Today, family names like the Peacocks and the Gills, well known in Richmond market in England so many centuries ago, the

Aldersons, Calverts, Harkers and so many others, have been absorbed into American life. They are the names of pioneers, men and women of courage who left their native villages so many years ago hoping only for a chance to work, to have some land and to build a home for their families and a future for their children. Their hopes must surely have been fulfilled and their contribution to developing a unique part of the American Middle West surely merits a place in the history of their time.

An Epilogue of People

IN ENDEAVOURING TO WRITE THIS STORY of emigration from the Yorkshire Dales, I have felt it right to avoid dwelling at too great a length on the experiences of many individual families. Rather have I tried to recount the story and its historical background in a manner that may encourage my readers, and especially those related to the early emigrants, to probe into their own family history and perhaps to take pride in the achievements of their forebears. Of course, much research has already been done and there are a number of well informed family history societies with interests on both sides of the Atlantic. But I have been made very aware that, though many letters and records have been lost in the course of time, there is still scope for much family detective work by those who may be interested and perhaps intrigued by the events of the past.

Information given to me about individual emigrants and their families has often been very detailed and authentic, sometimes scant, on occasions conflicting, and in other cases impossible to verify. The following brief notes from my records name some but by no means all of the men and women who emigrated between 1825 and 1850 to make a new life in America, mainly in the lead area of the Upper Mississippi. The majority of those I have named left from Swaledale but there are some who went from other dales of Northern England. Relatives of those listed may well have much additional information, and I recognise that some family records and opinions of events may sometimes differ in detail from the information I have recorded.

ALCOCK (or ALLCOCK) – Isaac and George are known to have emigrated in 1839. Both were married and had a number of children. They went to Platteville, Wisconsin and worked as miners. Ambrose Alcock and his wife probably emigrated at the same time, but they are said to have died of cholera in Galena, Illinois. Another Ambrose Alcock is mentioned as having been a preacher on the ship Roscius which left Liverpool with many dales people on board in 1849.

ALDERMAN – James Alderman came from a Nidderdale family and emigrated in the 1840s to live at Key West, near Dubuque, where he is known to have had 80 acres of land.

ALDERSON – A very large family name known in both Swaledale and Arkengarthdale. William and his wife Jane, sailed from Liverpool in 1833, John went in 1840 with his wife and two children to New Diggings. He was said to have been the discoverer of important lead deposits in the lucrative Champion Mine. Edmund Alderson emigrated in 1839, his brother Jonathan in 1842, and they both mined at New Diggings. By 1848, Jonathan was smelting lead with Simon Alderson, who had arrived a few years earlier. There were a number of other Alderson emigrants, and an Alderson Society now provides a source of information.

ALTON – Ann Alton and her husband left for America in 1839. Jane Alton of Gunnerside married W. H. CALVERT and left with him in 1849 to live in Benton, Wisconsin. After the death of her husband George, Hannah BUXTON (formerly Alton) emigrated at the late age of 57 years, with her daughter and son-in-law, John PEDLEY, and lived in Wisconsin.

ATKINSON – Archibald emigrated with his wife and son in 1834 and went to Hazel Green, Wisconsin. William left in 1840 and went to Council Hill, Illinois and later to Jefferson, Wisconsin (south-west of Benton). John emigrated in 1850 to join the others. Though there are some records of Atkinsons in Swaledale and also Wensleydale, they were and continue to be mainly an Arkengarthdale family.

AYRES – Joseph Ayres was a Yorkshire carpenter living in the New Diggings area in the early 1840s. He was employed by W. H. CALVERT to remodel the Methodist Church in Benton. It is thought that the spelling of the family may have been changed to

AYER(S) in later years for there are a number of gravestones with that spelling in Leadmine P. M. cemetery.

BAINBRIDGE – George and his wife Elizabeth are thought to have emigrated from Wensleydale with their first child in 1838. They had a further four children in the Middle West.

BARNINGHAM – James left for America in 1842 and worked as a smelter with Jonathan and Simon ALDERSON in Wisconsin.

BELL – Metcalfe Bell emigrated with his wife in 1830 and settled in Medina, Ohio. John and his wife Peggy emigrated in 1833 and went to Dubuque where he is said to have mined and then built up a dry goods business in which his son later became a partner. Later, James WALLIS and John RIDER, both dales immigrants, are said to have joined the business. Other Bells – James, William and Richard – emigrated to the area later in the century. It is likely that the Bells originated in Teesdale.

BLADES – William is thought to have emigrated to America before 1850 and to have served as a soldier in the Civil War. He was married and had a son and later William is known to have worked in Dubuque with H. B. Glover & Company.

BLENKIRON – Matthew emigrated from Swaledale in 1839 with a number of others from the dales. He went to Benton and later married Mary HARKER, aged only 15. They went to live in New Diggings. Matthew's widowed mother, Elizabeth, emigrated in 1850 aged 60 to join them. Thomas and Oliver Blenkiron went out to Dubuque but were later drowned in floods which beset Rockdale in 1876.

BLEWETT – John Blewett left Swaledale in 1843 with his wife Margaret and they went to live in Weston, Jo Davies County, Illinois.

BONSON – Robert and Mary emigrated from Swaledale in 1834, but Mary died of cholera travelling up the Mississippi River. Robert settled in Dubuque and with Richard WALLER and others, he erected the first blast furnace in America for smelting lead. His son Richard became prominent not only in mining but as a member of the state legislature, and an Inspector of Banks. He also had a major interest in the Dubuque and Pacific Railroad.

BRODERICK – One of the very earliest of Swaledale families. The diaries of Edward and James L. Broderick, who visited America in

39   *John and Mary Brunskill.*

1876, threw considerable light on the emigration of the lead mining families. George Broderick and his wife emigrated in 1849 with their baby Elizabeth, who died during the voyage.

BRUNSKILL – Joseph emigrated in 1833 and went to Akron, Ohio, and then to Dubuque. There he built a smelter in the Rockdale Valley which operated until late in the 19th century. Two of his sons, Joseph and James, are known to have worked in the family smelter. Joseph Sr. married twice and had 12 children by his first wife, Elizabeth WOODWARD. On her death he married a widow, Mrs Ann DAYKIN. Simon Brunskill emigrated in 1849 with his wife, who died travelling up the Mississippi. Simon went on to Dubuque with three children. Jane Brunskill married Henry CALVERT in Swaledale and they had three children when they emigrated, going first to New Diggings and then to Linden, Wisconsin. John Brunskill and his wife Mary were other members of the family known to have settled in the Dubuque area.

BUXTON – A name particularly connected with Gunnerside in Swaledale. Hannah Buxton emigrated in 1849 (see ALTON). John and Richard were also emigrant members of the family and John is recorded as having had a retail business in Leadmine, Wisconsin.

CALVERT – There are a number of families with this name and not all appear to be related. Benson Calvert is reported to have been in Jo Davies County in 1826 and George Calvert to have leased land for mining in the same year. Martin, Michael, Henry and Isiah all emigrated in the 1830s, probably from Arkengarthdale. Isiah is known to have lived in New Diggings. Henry Calvert was another dalesman to emigrate at that time with his wife Jane BRUNSKILL and their children. Henry's sister, Jane Calvert, married Edward HUGILL. Martin Calvert, who emigrated in 1839, is known to have married Ann ALDERSON of Reeth but he was later to die of pneumonia. William Harker Calvert from Swaledale who emigrated in 1839 returned to England 10 years later to marry Jane ALTON. William travelled back to America in 1849 and settled in Benton with his new wife. Jackson Calvert was a fellow passenger. Tom Calvert was a director of the Burrell Mining Company and James Calvert was one of the five directors of the Calvert Mining Company which had the lease of 215 acres on Calvert property near Benton. Probably the most famous Yorkshire Calvert was George who became Lord Baltimore (see chapter 'Who are the Americans?'). There is a Calvert memorial window in Benton Methodist Church.

CAYGILL – Christopher Caygill emigrated on the ship Saxony in 1849 with his younger brother William. William is thought to have returned later to England, married and then emigrated to Australia. Christopher travelled across the prairie from Galena to Linden, near Mineral Point, where he married and settled into farming (see also TIPLADY).

CLARKSON – Another respected old Swaledale family. Some members are known to have emigrated and settled in Dubuque including John who sailed in 1850 and later owned a 162 acre farm near Center Grove. Another emigrant from Swaledale at that time was James Clarkson who arrived in Dubuque with his wife Elizabeth.

CLEMINSON – Joseph emigrated in 1846 with his friend John LOCKEY from Feetham in Swaledale, and they went to Dubuque. William Cleminson, also from Feetham, went to Julien township, two miles west of Dubuque and on the north fork of Catfish Creek. There he built up 118 acres of farmland.

COATES – Leonard emigrated in 1836 and went to Platteville, where he and a friend built a smelter. William went with his parents in 1842; they were shipwrecked on Lake Erie but reached Dubuque, where they settled. After a visit to California, William returned, married Frances WALLER and set up a dry goods business. Simon Coates emigrated in 1849 and went to New Diggings. Tom also went out and became a blacksmith in Dubuque. Others in the area were Margaret, who, after the death of her first husband, married Matthew STOTT of Darlington, England, and there were Tom's sisters one of whom became Mrs James PRATT. There was a store in Dubuque known as Coates and Watters.

COTTINGHAM – An old Gunnerside family some of which are known to have emigrated and settled in the Dubuque area as well as in Benton where there is a Cottingham family window in the Methodist Church.

DAYKIN – Joseph and his wife Anne, emigrated in 1833; William left Gunnerside in 1849 with his wife Mary (METCALF) and went to Dubuque. They settled at Center Grove, Iowa, before going to

40 *The Christopher Metcalf Caygill homestead at Linden, Wisconsin with descendant Thomas Caygill and his family in the foreground.*

California. There they made money from gold mining and then returned to Center Grove, later settling in Benton. Ann Daykin had also emigrated (see BRUNSKILL), as did Elizabeth, who married Thomas LOCKEY.

DINSDALE – Stephen and Anne with their son Robert emigrated in 1839. Matthew went from Askrigg in Wensleydale in 1844 eventually reaching Linden and later Mineral Point. He had many experiences before travelling back to England to marry. When he returned to America, it was with his wife and elderly mother. Matthew eventually retired to Linden. His brother John and his wife emigrated to Wisconsin with Christopher CAYGILL in 1849 and also settled in Linden.

FAWCETT – Matthew Fawcett is reported to have been in Jo Davies County as early as 1826. The story of David and Ralph is noted in the chapter 'The Development of Dubuque'. There were other Fawcett emigrants, including Richard, who travelled with a large party of dales people in 1849, Leonard who went to South Dakota, and Edward who became a farmer near Key West, a few miles south of Dubuque.

GILL – Isiah Gill left Swaledale and sailed from Liverpool with his friend W. H. CALVERT and many others in 1839. He mined at New Diggings but died 10 years later. Richard and Mary Gill and five children emigrated in 1846 and went to Galena.

HARKER – John Harker's emigration to South America has been described in the chapter 'Southwards to Santander'. There were many Harkers in Swaledale and Wensleydale, several of whom emigrated to the Mississippi lead region, including James and Jane, who sailed in 1839. Amos and Simon were amongst the first to arrive at New Diggings. Joseph was the first storekeeper in Leadmine, near New Diggings. Solomon and his wife, formerly Nannie PEACOCK, emigrated in 1842 and went to live in Benton. Benjamin Harker went to East Liverpool, Ohio, and established a flourishing pottery works, the products being known as 'Harker Ware'. Later, as already noted, a Mrs Harker was reported to be teaching in the first school at Mineral Point as early as 1828.

HOLMES – John Holmes emigrated in 1830 with Metcalfe BELL and Anthony HUNT and worked initially in the Pennsylvanian coal mines.

HIRD – James was reported to have emigrated by 1848 and to be living in Jefferson, Wisconsin. Ten members of the Hird family are listed as having sailed from Liverpool in the following year. Some lived in Benton where they subscribed to a window in the Methodist Church, as did the BUXTON, W. H. CALVERT and COTTINGHAM families.

HUGILL – A James Hugill is said to have been in Jo Davies County in 1826 and Thomas Hugill was one of the first dalesmen to reach Platteville in 1828. Ambrose Hugill emigrated in that same year and, with Robert Waller, became a smelter in Galena. He returned to Swaledale in 1844 to marry Ann HARKER of Kearton and went back with his wife to Mineral Point. George Hugill was known to be in Platteville in 1834 and Edward Hugill, who married Jane CALVERT before leaving England, was there in 1836. Another George Hugill and his wife, Jane, left the Swaledale area for

America in 1845. George Hugill and his wife Ann were recorded as being in the town of Highland in 1850. A considerable family connection is recorded in the County census lists.

HUNT – Henry and his family went to Pennsylvania and the Schuykill country in 1830. Jonathan went with a large group of dales emigrants in 1849.

INGRAM – Richard Ingram emigrated from Swaledale in 1847 and lived at Benton.

JACKSON – Raw and Jane Jackson are known to have emigrated from Swaledale and are thought to have gone originally to the Galena area though they settled later on a farm at Orange near Cleveland, Ohio, where they are reported to have had 13 children.

KILBURN – Benjamin was known to be mining six miles north of Galena in 1833 where he was reported to have made a profitable strike of lead. He is recorded as having sold this strike and bought another lucrative mine at Langworthy Hollow in Dubuque County.

LAMBERT – Thomas and John from Aysgarth in Wensleydale emigrated in 1841. They were the sons of John, a woolcomber, and seemed to have settled in Wisconsin where Thomas is known to have owned 500 acres of prairie land.

LOCKEY – Thomas married Elizabeth DAYKIN and emigrated in 1839 with their children. They were reported to have gone to Julien township, near Dubuque. Later, Thomas was said to own a 120 acre farm near Center Grove as well as some mineral land near Dubuque. John Lockey went in 1846 from Gunnerside and settled with his wife, Mary, at Center Grove. He mined lead and then worked in smelters.

LONGSTAFF – Thomas Longstaff emigrated in 1839 and travelled with W. H. CALVERT and others to Galena and the Fever River area.

METCALFE (or METCALF) – John and his wife, formerly Betty TIPLADY, left for America in 1842 with Christopher PEACOCK and Solomon HARKER and his family. They are thought to have gone to the Benton area. Robert left in 1849, and Thomas Metcalfe formerly of Spring End, Swaledale, farmed 100 acres at Julien township, near Dubuque. The E and M Mine in the Fever River area is said to have been named after Elizabeth Metcalf, a Swaledale immigrant.

MILNER – James, Thomas and William left Swaledale in 1849 and went to either New Diggings or Dubuque.

MORTON – Joseph and James Morton emigrated from Swaledale with Thomas ROBINSON in 1844. They were miners and settled in New Diggings.

NATTRASS – Cuthbert and his wife Mary Jane emigrated in the early 1840s and went to Wisconsin.

PARKIN – Broderick Parkin was a Swaledale emigrant, reported to have emigrated in the 1840s and to have settled in the Dubuque area.

PEACOCK – Thomas Peacock was referred to as being one of the first to arrive at New Diggings. Christopher Peacock, his wife, Peggy, and four children left for America in 1842 and William emigrated in 1839 on the same boat as W. H. CALVERT and many others. He was known to go to Council Hill. Robert Peacock and George, with his wife and children, went in 1849. Nannie Peacock married Solomon HARKER and they emigrated to America in 1842.

PEDLEY (or PEDELTY) – John Pedley went in 1849 with his wife and her mother, Hannah BUXTON. William and his wife also went and settled in New Diggings. Peter and Mary his wife and three children are known to have emigrated in 1845 and they lived in New Diggings.

POUNDER – John Pounder is known to have left Swaledale for America in 1830 having been given £20 by the Church – a Select Vestry payment.

PRATT – James Pratt emigrated with his wife, Hannah, in 1833 (see chapter headed 'Swaledale goes to Dubuque'). James is recorded as having built the Rockdale flour mill with a partner in 1840. Another James, and Metcalf Pratt sailed out on the Saxony in 1849 (see also the RAW family).

RAISBECK – John Raisbeck and his wife formerly Jane BAINBRIDGE emigrated from Arkengarthdale in 1850 with their eight children and went to Benton, Wisconsin. John was first a miner and then a farmer of repute. His eldest son Robert, with his wife formerly Ruth

ADDISON, also emigrated and went to New Diggings. The family became known for their development of the Raisbeck Mine.

RAW (or ROWE) – George and Ann, his wife, emigrated in 1839 with
their infant daughter, Hannah. George seems to have worked in the mines and then took up farming in the Dubuque area. Anthony and Melissa Raw went at the same time and were later said to be living at Council Hill with their six children. Martin Luther Raw went from Whitaside, Swaledale in 1849 with his wife, formerly Ann SPENSLEY. They had ten children two of whom had married into the Pratt family. James Raw and his wife, formerly Mary ALDERSON, also emigrated at this time and are said to have had eight children. There is a particularly large Raw family connection in America and there are links with the PRATT family as well as the SPENSLEYS.

REYNOLDSON – George Reynoldson, an emigrant from Swaledale in 1845, set up a smelter in the Dubuque area as well as a tanning yard and leather store. Joseph Reynoldson who emigrated at the same time, had 16 acres of mineral land in Julien township.

RICHARDSON – Joseph Richardson married Elizabeth WATTERS, daughter of a lead miner from Kearton in Swaledale. They left in 1845 and travelled via the Mississippi River to reach New Diggings where Joseph worked in the mines before taking up farming.

RIDER – (see BELL).

ROBINSON – William left the dales for America in 1834, Joseph emigrated in 1841 and went to Platteville. Thomas went in 1844 with his wife Ann and their children and settled in New Diggings.

SHEPHERD – Anthony left in the late 1840s from Sedbergh. He married Mary Ann PEDLEY (or Pedelty) of Swaledale. They settled in Platteville and had nine children.

SIMPSON – Nathan Simpson emigrated and went to Dubuque, where he worked in smelting.

SPENSLEY – Martin Spensley is said to have been the first of this large family to settle in America. He is recorded as living in Galena in 1830. John and Ralph were in the area by 1834, and Martin, Mason, Richard, James and William were all there by 1839. John and Harker Spensley emigrated in 1849 with their wives, and all are said to have settled in the Fever River area or in Dubuque, several being involved in smelting. A smelting concern, Spensley & Co was established in Mineral Point and Mason and Ralph Spensley formed a partnership with others in 1850 to operate a smelter near Dubuque. Later, records show that there was a firm of Dubuque lawyers known as Spensley and Spensley.

THWAITES – Tom Thwaites was another Swaledale man who was said to have gone to Dubuque by 1850.

TIPLADY – A very old dales family with a history which goes back 600 years. Thought to be of Swaledale origin they also had a long connection with Askrigg and Gayle in Wensleydale. They have links with the CAYGILL family going back to the year 1687 when Ralph Tiplady married Elizabeth Caygill. Some of the Tiplady family are known to have been Quakers. Of those who emigrated, Betty Tiplady, who married John METCALFE, emigrated with him to the Dubuque area in 1842. Betty's sister, Mary Tiplady from Spring End, Gunnerside married George WHARTON who came from Satron in Swaledale. They also settled near Dubuque.

WAISTILL – Thomas, from Hoggarths Farm in Swaledale Head emigrated in 1842 and settled in Shullsburg, Wisconsin where he died.

WALLER – Robert Waller went to America from Whitaside in Swaledale in 1828 and became a smelter at Galena. His daughter, Frances, married William COATES. Richard ('Dickey') Waller emigrated with his wife Mary in 1834 and it is said that, together with his brother Robert and Richard BONSON, 'Dickey' built the first blast furnace in America. At the time of James BRODERICK'S visit to Dubuque in 1877, Dickey Waller was known to be alive and aged 81 years.

WALLIS – William Wallis was an emigrant who settled in New Diggings where he became Clerk to the Board of Supervisors in the township. James married Ann BELL, emigrated to Dubuque in 1843 and he went into partnership with John Bell and John RIDER in a dry goods business.

WATTERS – A family connection built up in the Dubuque area. John built a smelter near Rockdale and other members of the family recorded are Tom and his wife Nanny and young John who arrived with his wife Nancy in 1849 (see also RICHARDSON). Tom Watters later worked in the Rockdale flour mill built in 1840 by James PRATT and his partner from Scotland, Walter MANSON. It is known that, when Tom died, his widow lived in Table Mound township, two miles south of Center Grove. William Watters is known to have owned 141 acres of land in Table Mound township, north of Center Grove (see also RICHARDSON).

WHARTON – George Wharton emigrated to the Dubuque area from Satron in Swaledale and married Mary TIPLADY who had been living at Spring End, Gunnerside.

WILLIS – Matthew Willis of Carperby in Wensleydale emigrated in 1845 with his family, and he later settled on a 470 acre farm near Mineral Point.

WISEMAN – Christopher Wiseman emigrated from Swaledale with his wife, Elizabeth, in 1845 and they went to Galena. Henry, his brother, followed via the Mississippi River in 1848. Charles and his wife Elizabeth and children also emigrated to the Fever River area in 1845.

WOODWARD – William Woodward left Yorkshire in 1833 and worked at first in the coal mines of Pennsylvania. Sarah Woodward married Edmund ALDERSON (see ALDERSON) and went to New Diggings. Other Woodwards settled in the Dubuque area and are known to have owned mineral land near Center Grove.

References

IN COMPILING THIS BOOK I have been helped by being able to talk and correspond with a number of people with Yorkshire Dales connections living on both sides of the Atlantic and the study of a number of family letters and records has produced much information.

Apart from the valuable thesis written by Dr John Thornton Dixon which has already been acknowledged, reference has been made to the following publications for historical and other information. The various titles are listed in three sections, and provide a source of further reading if required.

SWALEDALE HISTORY

Swaledale by Ella Pontefract (J. M. Dent – 1934)

A History of Swaledale by Edmund Cooper (Dalesman –1973)

Men of Swaledale by Edmund Cooper (Clapham - 1960)

A History of Richmond and Swaledale by Fieldhouse and Jennings (Phillimore – 1978)

The Old Hand Knitters of the Dales by Marie Hartley and Joan Ingilby (Dalesman 1978)

Poverty and Treatment of Poverty in the North Riding of Yorkshire 1780-1847 by R. P. Hastings (thesis – University of York)

Gunnerside Chapel and Gunnerside Folk by M. Batty (Teesdale 1967)

The Industrial Revolution in Swaledale Lead Mining by B. Jennings (British Speleological Association – 1963)

The Lead Smelting Mills of the Yorkshire Dales and Northern Pennines by Robert T. Clough (published by the Author 1980)

The Smelting of Lead Ores, from 'Forster's Strata' by Westgarth Forster (Andrew Reid, London – 1883)

EMIGRATION

Liverpool and The Mersey 1700-1970 by Francis E. Hyde (David and Charles 1971)

Emigration to America 1800 – 1850 by Susan Matthews (York thesis – 1967)

The Great Migration by E. C. Guillet (Nelson – 1937)

Emigration from the U.K. to North America by Stanley C. Johnson (London – 1913)

American Immigration by M. A. Jones (Chicago Press – 1960)

History of Immigration to the United States by William J. Bramwell (Radfield, New York – 1856)

Invisible Immigrants by Charlotte Erickson (Leicester University Press, 1972)

AMERICAN HISTORY AND THE LEAD AREA OF THE UPPER MISSISSIPPI

The Growth of the American Republic by Morison, Commager and Leuchtenburg (Oxford University Press 1980, (Volume 1)

The United States of America by Hugh Brogan (Pelican 1986)

American Notes by Charles Dickens (Nelson 1904)

The Settlement of the Lead Mining Region by John Le Roy Grindell (The State Historical Society of Wisconsin)

The Wisconsin Lead Region by Schafer (Madison – 1932)

The Metallurgy of Argentiferous Lead by M. Eissler (1891)

The Character of the Country edited by Loren N. Horton (Iowa State Historical Dept. – 1976)

Dubuque on the Mississippi 1788-1988 by William E. Wilkie (Loras Press)

The History of Dubuque County, Iowa (Chicago, Western Historical Company 1880)

Portrait and Biographical Record of Dubuque by Jones and Clayton (Chicago, Chapman Publishing Co., 1894)

Dubuque County History (Iowa writer project, W.P.A., 1942)

How Rogers Clark won the North West (Chicago, A. C. McClurg & Co., 1903)

The Mines of Spain by A. P. Shiras (Annals (3), v, 321-334, April 1902)

The Galena Lead District by James E. Wright (Madison-University of Wisconsin – 1966)

New Diggings on the Fever 1824-1864 and
New Diggings is an Old Diggings by Margaret S. Carter (1959)

Index